The Wall Tiling Book

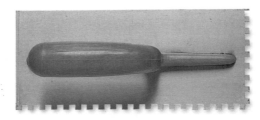

Alex Portelli

Contents

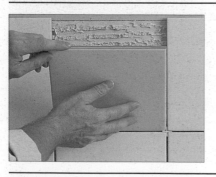

Introduction

Ceramic wall tiles have been used for many centuries, and there is no better testimony to their usefulness and durability. Despite the advent of many wonderful modern materials, the glazed clay tile is still the most practical means of providing a wall with an attractive, easily cleaned, hard-wearing, waterproof surface that will keep its appearance, come what may. These properties are essential in parts of bathrooms and kitchens, and are also useful in cloakrooms, toilets, and utility rooms.

In recent years there has been a steady increase in the number of people prepared to tackle home improvement jobs themselves rather than employ professionals. Keeping step with this movement, manufacturers and suppliers have made materials and tools designed for the amateur rather than professional, often simplifying jobs in the process. This, in turn, has encouraged even more householders to 'do it themselves'.

However, tiling is not quite as simple as it might at first seem, and to produce a professional finish requires considerable skill. That is not to say that amateurs cannot produce good tiling, but it requires care and patience, and an understanding of what you are doing and why.

The following chapters take you through all the necessary techniques, tips and facts needed to tile a wall successfully. If you use the information set out in this book and take time and care, there is no reason why you should not achieve excellent results.

Ideas and Choices

There is a wealth of wall tiles to choose from in a wide range of colours, patterns, textures and sizes. Most are ceramic, but you can also find marble tiles, and mosaics in a variety of other materials. As a result, no matter what the style of decor in your bathroom, kitchen, cloakroom or bedroom, you will be able to find the right tiles for the job.

Take your time when deciding on a tiling scheme; wall tiles are not only more expensive than other forms of decoration, but they are also more difficult to change if you are not happy with them. It is essential to find a scheme that you can live with for a long time. If in doubt, opt for something simple that will provide a neutral backdrop rather than a design that will become a major visual feature. You may find inspiration in magazines, other people's homes, tile brochures, displays at tile suppliers, or even the patterns in wallpapers or fabrics.

Classical influence

The use of tiles and mosaics in bathrooms dates back many, many centuries. They are the most practical means of giving the walls – and floors – an attractive, waterproof surface. Used with care, and combined with carefully chosen bathroom fittings, they can give a bathroom a timeless, classical look.

One important consideration, regardless of the style of your bathroom, is to use large tiles when tiling a large area, such as a wall or even a complete room. These produce a far less 'busy' looking surface, and in a small room actually help to make it look larger. Reserve small tiles for small areas such as splashbacks.

◄ Although coloured bathroom suites come into and go out of fashion, white fittings and white tiles never seem to date. However, a large expanse of white tiles can look very cold and uninteresting; you need to add some form of accent to focus the eye. In this particular case, the walls have been divided into horizontal panels by contrasting rows of tiles in blues and greys.

At waist height, a dado has been formed by adding a row of patterned tiles that are designed for this very purpose. They are the same size as the field tiles, making setting out easy (see pages 32–35). Up to dado height, the latter are fixed conventionally, being aligned both horizontally and vertically. Above the dado, the rows of tiles run diagonally to give a diamond pattern.

This continues to picture-rail height, where a darker band of tiles gives more definition. It comprises narrow, dark blue pencil tiles, a row of alternating, small dark blue and white tiles, and a row of blue moulded dado tiles. From this 'picture rail' upwards, the white tiles continue to the ceiling in normal fashion.

At floor level, the 'picture rail' is echoed by a row of pencil tiles and a row of small blue and white tiles.

Using horizontal accents in this fashion not only breaks up a large expanse of tiles, but also allows you to change the fixing pattern on part of the wall for added interest.

◄ Marble or simulated marble tiles (which can look very realistic) are ideal for creating a classically elegant bathroom. With the careful positioning of inset tiles and/or dados or borders, you can give an air of stylish opulence. By using a contrasting colour of tile to form a floor-to-ceiling panel behind the basin and mirror, warmth and interest have been added to this bathroom, which could have looked quite bland if the pale tiles had been used throughout.

The inset tiles below the lights on the adjacent wall provide additional visual interest and prevent this area from being dominated by the darker colour.

Many marble tiles are quite large in size, and this bathroom illustrates the benefit of using large tiles rather than small ones when tiling complete walls, particularly in a small room. Small tiles produce a surface that looks much busier and actually emphasises the smallness of a room; large tiles have the opposite effect.

► Although the strong colour of these splashback tiles contrasts effectively with the tiles used throughout the rest of the bathroom, the edge of the panel has been given further definition by adding patterned dado/border tiles.

Black and white

The stark contrast between black and white tiles can be used to good effect in both bathrooms and kitchens, whether the black tiles are used to provide simple accents, or more boldly in large areas. Far from producing a gloomy feel, large areas of black tiles suggest an air of luxury and style. They can be particularly effective when used with a high-tech bathroom suite and lots of chromium-plated or stainless steel accessories.

◀ Tiling in black and white has been traditional in bathrooms for years; the black tiles usually being included as accents to break up an overall white scheme. However, larger areas of black tiles can be used to make dramatic statements, as in this small bathroom. Here they form a backdrop for the toilet and clad the panelling around the bath.

To add further interest, white tiles with simple black patterns have been used to make rectangular outlines on the white background. Patterns like this benefit from careful pre-planning, and a sketch plan would be essential to determine the positions of the various decorative elements for the most effective arrangement (see pages 30–31).

► Using tiles of one colour for a splashback, whether in the kitchen or bathroom, can look boring, particularly if they are white. However, you need not necessarily resort to colour to provide visual interest. This all-white splashback is enlivened by a dado tile with a moulded relief pattern. The shapes in the pattern are picked out by light and shade, and will change with the lighting conditions, adding a subtle accent to the splashback.

◄ Purpose-made dado tiles are often a different size to the field tiles that surround them, so there is no point in trying to keep all the joints aligned. Instead, the joints should be deliberately staggered so that they don't align anywhere.

Using standard tiles of different sizes together, however, can present problems. This striking black and white splashback, for example, is made up of 10cm (4in)-square black tiles, but the dado running through the centre comprises 20cm (8in)-square tiles with a printed chequer pattern.

Although these dado tiles are twice the width of the field tiles, this makes no allowance for the grout joint between the two smaller tiles. Consequently, for all the joints to line up, it would have been necessary either to allow wider joints between the large tiles, or narrower joints than normal between the smaller ones, or a combination of the two. Careful setting out is essential, and suitable pieces of card should be used to space the tiles.

Country style

The wide variety of tiles available makes it possible to match any decor scheme imaginable: from simple rustic to high-tech futuristic. No matter what the style of the room, there will be tiles to fit right in. For the former, subdued tones are best, particularly when teamed with old-fashioned bathroom suites and natural-finish wooden cabinets. The tiles should make a pleasing, but unobtrusive backdrop to the fittings and accessories in the room, providing a sense of harmony and softness.

◄ Half-tiling bathroom walls can often be as effective as tiling them completely, and it reduces the overall cost of the job. The tiles provide an easily cleaned, water-resistant surface for the area of the walls that is likely to be splashed from the basin or bath.

Tiles should be fixed to the wall up to dado (waist) height – or at least high enough above the basin to provide an effective splashback. When setting out, choose the dado height and mark off the wall downwards, starting with a whole tile at the top. Unless the floor is completely level, position the dado line to leave a cut tile of between one- and two-thirds at the bottom.

Although you can leave the edges of the top tiles showing – if glazed – it is much more effective to add a proper dado of some form. You can use dado tiles or, as here, a wooden moulding.

◄ Splashbacks, whether in the kitchen or bathroom, offer fewer opportunities than complete walls when it comes to setting out complex designs, and in any event, too busy a pattern or tiling layout could look out of place. However, a splashback need not be restricted purely to one type and colour of tile. With a little imagination, attractive arrangements can be achieved.

Here, for example, a horizontal row of alternating blue and pale green tiles at worktop level is divided from the rest of the diagonally tiled beige splashback by a half-round dado moulding in blue and green. To add interest to the taller area of tiles behind the hob, a simple diamond motif has been incorporated using two blue and two green tiles.

When a dado is incorporated in a kitchen splashback in this manner, it is best to fix it one tile above the worktop. In this position it will not be shielded from the eye by the cupboards above, and usually it won't interfere with any electrical outlets set in the wall.

◄ To add visual interest to this tiled splashback, rather than running a dado through it, the taller area of tiles behind the hob has been given a simple diagonally tiled panel outlined by moulded dado tiles. Notice how the joints of the dado tiles, which are longer than the field tiles, have been staggered in relation to them.

The ends of the dado tiles have also been mitred at the corners. This is best done with a tile saw.

Bold colours

Many would prefer a tiled surface to be subtle in appearance and form a neutral backdrop to other features in the room, but the bold use of strongly coloured tiles can produce eye-catching effects with dramatic impact. In such cases, the tiles become the major decorative feature, so care must be taken to select colours and patterns that will stand the test of time: changing wallpaper and paint that have become outdated is easy, but changing tiles is much more complex and expensive.

With such schemes, it is certainly worth drawing up a paper plan before tiling. When you have decided on the scheme you want, put the plan away for a week or so, then come back to it to see if you have changed your mind. Once the tiles are on the wall, you will have to live with them.

◄ Although it is generally much better to use large tiles when tiling a large area, particularly complete walls, small mosaics can also be very effective. The reason for this is that the individual mosaic pieces are so small that the eye does not immediately recognise them individually. Instead, especially when a random combination of colours is chosen such as this, the wall takes on a pleasing mottled appearance. These glass mosaics come in a wide variety of quite intense colours that would look garish in larger pieces.

Another advantage of small mosaics is that they are ideal for tiling a curved surface.

▶ A splashback can often accommodate a pattern or colour combinations that would be too overwhelming on a larger scale. These two strong blues, for example, make a striking, but simple, statement so that the splashback becomes a strong visual element in the decor of the kitchen. This is helped by the subdued colouring of the cabinets and worktop.

Take care with this type of colour scheme, however, as if teamed with strongly coloured cabinets or worktop, it could result in visual chaos.

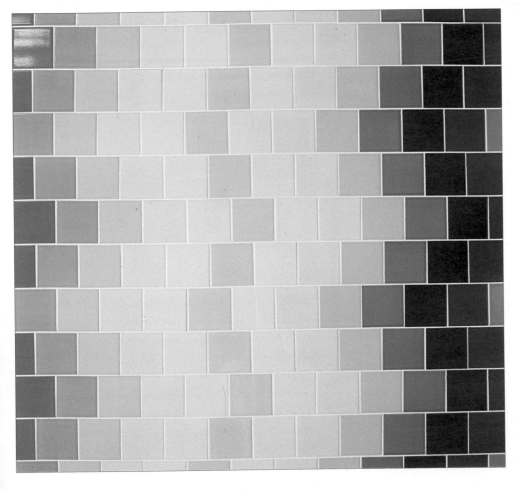

◀ Giving rein to your imagination can produce some stunning combinations of tiles. Here, a range of plain colours has been combined to produce a dramatic graduated effect. While not to everyone's taste perhaps, it would make a powerful feature in a bathroom.

Types of tile

No matter what you want to tile – be it a small splashback behind a handbasin in a bedroom or a complete bathroom – the choice of tiles available is vast. For the widest selection, visit a tile specialist, who will also be able to advise you on the quantities you need together with any other essential materials. Sizes vary from small mosaics, of about 25mm (1in) square, up to large marble and ceramic tiles measuring 300mm (12in) square or even 400 x 250mm (16 x 10in).

An important consideration is whether the tiles you want have glazed or unglazed edges. With the latter, unless you are tiling a wall from end to end and top to bottom, or a splashback that is bordered on all four sides in some way, you will need a means of concealing the edges around the perimeter of the tiled area. Fortunately, special border tiles are made just for this purpose, or you can use plastic tile trim or a wooden moulding.

STANDARD

These ceramic wall tiles offer a wide range of colours, patterns and sizes from which to choose. Invariably, they are square, but you can also find oblong examples that can be fixed in a brick-like pattern for extra interest. Smaller tiles are best used for splashbacks rather than large ones. Some of these are particularly dense, having been fired to higher temperatures than for ordinary wall tiles. This creates a hard, glazed surface suitable for kitchen worktop use.

MOSAICS AND INSERTS

Mosaics are simply small tiles, the largest being a little over 50mm (2in) square. They usually come in sheets on either a mesh backing or with a paper facing that holds the individual tiles together. Their small size makes them ideal for splashbacks. Moreover, sheets of the smallest mosaics can be fixed to curved surfaces with little trouble.

Another form of small tile is the insert, a simple coloured square that is designed to fit at the point where the corners of four tiles meet. These provide a simple means of breaking up a large expanse of plain tiles. Special tiles with one corner cut off accommodate the inserts.

HAND-PAINTED

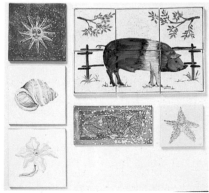

Most patterned tiles have printed designs on them, but you can also obtain hand-painted tiles, which offer unique motifs. These make wonderful insets, adding visual appeal to an otherwise plain area of tiling. No two hand-painted designs will ever be the same, which is part of their appeal.

Occasionally, several tiles will be used to form a larger picture. These can be positioned in much the same manner as a conventional picture, possibly outlined with border or dado tiles.

BORDERS AND DADOS

From narrow pencil tiles – about 13mm (½in) wide – to deep picture tiles, borders and dados come in a variety of sizes, colours, patterns and shapes. Although normally fixed in horizontal bands to break up or frame a large expanse of plain tiles, they can also be used vertically. Alternatively, they can be employed to frame panels of tiles in contrasting colours or tiling patterns. Those with moulded relief patterns will bring an added dimension of shape to a scheme.

MARBLE AND MOORISH

Genuine marble and simulated marble tiles allow you to create classically inspired tiling schemes. Because genuine marble tiles are very expensive, one way of achieving an effective finish is to use simulated marble field tiles for most of the work with genuine marble borders and dados as visual accents.

For a more exotic appearance, you can also choose tiles inspired by Moorish designs.

INSETS AND FEATURES

You will also find special tiles that can be used as visual accents in a tiling scheme. Inset tiles, for example, come in standard sizes, but bear a central motif. They can be fixed at random or in a regular pattern among plain tiles. In some cases, two or more tiles will fit together to make a larger picture.

Hand-made tiles from countries such as Africa and Mexico can provide extra interest, being uneven in shape and having a lovely mellow appearance with hand-painted designs. Some have an imitation crackle effect to give an antique look.

Preparation

Before carrying out any wall tiling work – whether a simple splashback behind a basin or a complete room – it is essential that the surface to be tiled is sound and flat.

Tiles can be applied to a variety of wall surfaces: plaster, plasterboard, cement render, plywood, painted surfaces, and even over old ceramic tiles. However, to ensure a successful job, the surface must be dry, dust-free and completely stable.

If necessary, take steps to prepare the surface, removing any irregularities, weaknesses and unevenness. In extreme cases, you may even have to strip the plaster from a wall and either replaster it or clad the exposed masonry with plasterboard. Don't skimp on this stage of the job; investing time and effort in preparation will pay dividends later.

Tools and materials

Even if you only intend tiling a small splashback, you will need a few special tiling tools to complete the job. Once you have the basics, you can add tools for specific jobs if and when you need them. You will also need a few general-purpose tools, such as can be found in most household tool kits.

The materials required for tiling will depend on the job itself. In some cases, other than the tiles, all you will need is the appropriate adhesive, grout and tile spacers.

PREPARATION

Cold chisel
For chipping out damaged tiles and old adhesive

Filling knife
For removing wallpaper and loose paint; filling cracks and holes

Steel float
For filling large areas of damaged plaster

Sanding block
Silicone carbide paper
For keying surface of old tiles for new tile adhesive

Glasspaper
For sanding down filler when preparing walls

Screwdriver Paintbrush   Hammers

TILING

Spirit level

Tape measure

Small trowel
For scooping adhesive on to wall and grout on to tiles

Masking tape
Prevents drill bit from skidding off tile

Electric drill
For drilling tiles when removing them or attaching pipe clips, etc

Junior hacksaw
Cuts plastic corner trim and bath-sealing strip

Sealant dispenser
Use when applying silicone sealant

Craft knife
Cuts mesh backing of mosaics

Notched adhesive spreader

Grout spreader (squeegee)

Grout shaper
Finishes grout joints neatly

Clean cloth

Sponge

Plastic scouring pad
Removes excess epoxy grout from worktop tiles

Tile scorer/grout raker
For scoring tiles when cutting or removing old grout

Toothed grout raker
Removes old grout from narrow joints

Tile-cutting tools

Tile spike
For scoring tiles when cutting

Combined cutting wheel/snapper
Scores and snaps tiles

Tile-cutting machine
Measures, scores and cuts tiles

Nibblers
Removes narrow strips or waste from intricate shapes

Tile saw
Cuts intricate shapes or moulded tiles

Tile file
For cleaning up edges of tiles after cutting

MATERIALS

Bath trim
Makes a waterproof joint between the bath and wall, the tiles being fixed over its vertical lip

Cross-shaped tile spacers
Ensures uniform joints between tiles

Plastic corner trim
For finishing external corners of walls and edges of splashbacks when using tiles with unglazed edges

PERSONAL PROTECTION

Thick gloves
Protects hands when chipping out tiles

Safety goggles
Protects eyes from flying fragments of tile when chipping out

ADHESIVE

Adhesive for fixing ceramic tiles to walls is available both ready-mixed, and in powder form for mixing with water. The former is more convenient to use, but the latter is less expensive and may be worth considering for a large job. Various quantities are available, and coverage is specified on the container.

There are two basic types of adhesive:

All-purpose

A water-resistant adhesive suitable for use in kitchens and bathrooms. Some all-purpose adhesives can also be employed as grout, but make sure that this is specified on the container before using it in this way.

Waterproof

Use in areas where the tiles are subjected to regular and substantial soaking in water, such as shower cubicles.

GROUT

Grout comes as a powder for mixing with water or ready-mixed. A hardener must be added to epoxy grout before it can be used. White grout is the most common, but a range of colours is also available. The container will specify the coverage you can expect. Various types are available:

Standard

Use where the tiles are unlikely to come into contact with water.

Water-resistant

For splashbacks and general kitchen and bathroom tiling.

Waterproof

Use where the tiles will be subjected to regular and substantial soaking, such as shower cubicles.

Epoxy

A very hard grout that is waterproof and will not harbour germs. Use for kitchen worktops.

Types of surface

In many cases, you may want to tile a wall that was previously painted or papered. Tiles can be applied directly over gloss and emulsion paint, provided the underlying plaster and the paint itself are sound. The minimum of preparation work will be necessary prior to tiling. However, walls that have an old-fashioned distemper finish should be stripped completely, as distemper is notoriously unstable. Wash it off with water and a little wallpaper stripper, then seal the surface with a stabilising solution.

Old wallpaper should be stripped completely. Whether you use the traditional soak-and-scrape method, as illustrated below, or a steam stripper, make sure the wall has dried completely before tiling.

TOOLS: Bucket, sponge, wallpaper scraper, sanding block, large paintbrush, hammer, cold chisel, small trowel, wooden batten

MATERIALS: Wallpaper stripper, glasspaper, sugar soap, stabilising solution/ tile adhesive primer, ready-mixed mortar/one-coat plaster, silicone carbide paper

PREPARING THE WALL

1 If the wall was papered originally, soak the paper with a solution of wallpaper stripper, and scrape it off. Vinyl types should be peeled off and their backing paper stripped to expose the plaster. Similarly, remove any lining paper.

2 On painted surfaces, rub down any flaking paint with coarse glasspaper until you have a sound finish. To help the tiles stick to the wall, key the paint by scoring with a scraper. Wash down with a sugar-soap solution to remove dust and grease.

3 Whatever the surface, it should be sealed with a proprietary stabilising solution, such as PVA sealant or tile adhesive primer. Dilute this and apply according to the manufacturer's instructions. Allow to dry completely.

OLD CERAMIC TILES

You can re-tile directly on top of existing ceramic tiling, provided the tiles are firmly attached to the wall and offer a reasonably flat surface. If possible, arrange the positions of the new tiles so that they overlap the joints of the old; this will produce a stronger result.

1 If any of the original tiles are broken, loose or hollow-sounding, carefully rake out the surrounding grout using a nail and chip them out with a hammer and cold chisel. Dampen the wall behind and fill the recess with either mortar or plaster.

2 Make the mortar or plaster exactly level with the surrounding tiles by working a small wooden batten across the area with a gentle sawing action. If necessary, fill any depressions with more mortar or plaster. Check that it is level again and allow it to dry completely.

3 Although the surface of ceramic tiles should provide a sound enough base for the new tiles, you can make doubly sure by rubbing them down with silicone carbide paper. This will scratch the glaze, providing an effective key for the tile adhesive.

4 Finally, wash the tiles down thoroughly with soapy water to remove all traces of dust and grease. Make sure they are completely dry before beginning to add the new tiles.

Cracks and holes

It is essential to have a flat surface on which to apply tiles. Although tile adhesive can accommodate depressions in the wall of up to 6mm (¼in), any significant undulation will be reflected in the finished tiled surface. It is a good idea to check the flatness of the wall with a long wooden straight edge, running it up the wall and along it.

Small bumps can be hammered down and any resulting depressions filled. Low areas can also be filled; if necessary, deepen them and replaster. If the wall is very uneven, it may pay to apply a skim of fresh plaster or even to panel the wall with plasterboard.

Minor cracks in plaster can be left, but fill large ones. Any loose areas of plaster should be hacked off and the area replastered or filled.

TOOLS: Steel rule, hammer, filling knife, old paintbrush, small trowel, bolster chisel, steel float, short wooden batten, sanding block

MATERIALS: Filler, one-coat plaster or ready-mixed mortar, coarse glasspaper, masonry nails, stabilising solution/tile adhesive primer

1 Major cracks in plasterwork should be filled. First, work the corner of the filling knife blade along the crack to undercut the edges (so that the filler can grip well), then brush out all the dust and loose debris. Use an old paintbrush to dampen the crack and press filler into it with the knife. Dampen the straight edge of the blade and use it to level the filler with the surrounding wall.

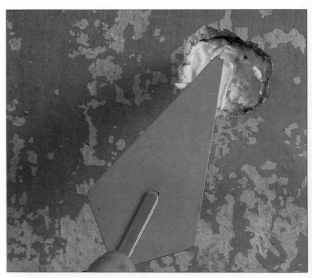

2 Filler won't dry properly if it is applied too thickly, so deep holes must be filled in two or more stages. Use a small trowel to insert an initial layer, using the point to work it down into the crevices at the bottom of the hole.

3 When the first layer of filler has dried, add another layer with a filling knife, pressing it in well and striking it off level with the surrounding plaster.

4 Do not worry about minor damage to external corners, as the tiles and/or corner trim will bridge any slight gap. However, where substantial portions of the plaster are missing, the corner should be built up with filler or one-coat plaster. Temporarily nail a batten to one edge to provide a support for the filler.

5 Check that the plaster is in contact with the wall by rapping it with your knuckles; where it has come away from the backing you will hear a hollow sound. Chop these areas away with a bolster chisel and hammer, undercutting the edges. Then fill with one-coat plaster or mortar, levelling it with the surrounding plaster using a wooden batten.

6 Allow any filled areas to dry completely, then rub them down with coarse glasspaper wrapped around a sanding block. You do not need to achieve the perfect surface that you would need for painting, but the filled area must be level with the surrounding surface. Finally, seal the wall with a stabilising solution or tile adhesive primer.

Boxing in and panelling

Wherever possible, pipes that run down or along walls should be concealed by boxing them in, and the resulting box tiled as usual. You can panel the box with plasterboard, MDF, or marine-grade plywood where damp conditions are expected. A rigid construction is essential to avoid cracking of the grout between the tiles, so use screws rather than nails to hold it together. Where the box conceals a hot water pipe, insulate the pipe to contain the heat; otherwise, it may cause the wood to shrink, again causing cracking.

All wooden surfaces should be sealed with a solvent-based primer prior to tiling.

TOOLS: Steel tape measure, pencil, saw, bradawl, electric drill, wood bit, masonry bit, countersink bit, screwdriver

MATERIALS: 50 x 25mm (2 x 1in)/25mm (1in) battens, 12 or 19mm (½ or ¾in) marine-grade plywood/MDF/plasterboard, countersunk screws, wall plugs

CONCEALING PIPES

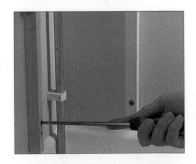

1 Where pipes run down a corner of the room, fix 25mm (1in)-square vertical battens to each wall, securing them with countersunk screws driven into wall plugs. Position the battens so that the size of the finished box won't require any cut tiles.

2 Cut two sections of 19mm (¾in)-thick marine-grade plywood or MDF to the correct size, and butt-joint them along their outer edges, using countersunk screws. Then screw the assembled panels to the battens already fixed on the wall.

BOXING PIPES

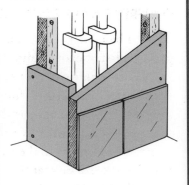

A separate framework will not be necessary if you use board butt-joined at the corner, screwed to battens.

PANELLING A BATH

1 A bath can be made to look an integral part of a bath-room if it is given a tiled surround.

The procedure is essentially the same as boxing in pipes: a wooden framework is built around the bath and panelled in ready for tiling. Construct a framework around the bath, using 50 x 25mm (2 x 1in) wooden battens. Screw them to the adjacent walls and floor to provide a rigid structure. Many acrylic and fibreglass baths have wooden reinforcing around the edge, and the frame can be screwed to this as well. Alternatively, make the framework slightly lower than the bath so that you can tile under the lip.

2 Panel the framework with 12mm (½in) marine-grade plywood, attaching it with countersunk screws. Make sure the screw heads are below the surface, as otherwise they will get in the way of the tiles and make the surface uneven.

3 At the tap and waste outlet end, make up an access panel, or purchase a ready-made double-lipped access panel, securing it with magnetic catches. The panel must be large enough for you to reach all the plumbing. After tiling, disguise the edges of the panel with silicone sealant, which will still allow the panel's removal.

COVERING BARE BRICK WALLS

To tile a bare brick wall it can be plastered, but it will be quicker to panel it plasterboard, 12mm (½in) plywood or MDF sheets.

First, fix framework to the wall, using 50 x 25mm (2 x 1in) vertical battens spaced no further apart than 30cm (12in). In addition, horizontal battens should run along the top and bottom of the wall. Frame window and door openings completely.

Screw the battens to the wall, using a long straight edge and a spirit level to ensure that they are all in line from top to bottom and perfectly vertical. If necessary, pack behind them with scraps of wood. Then fix the panels using countersunk screws.

When using plywood as a base for tiling, choose a waterproof type in case moisture should seep through any of the joints. This is essential when constructing a shower cubicle.

Planning and Setting Out

Careful planning and setting out are crucial to the success of any tiling job. You need to decide on the type and size of tiles you want, determine how many to buy, work out how they will be arranged on the wall for the best visual effect, and choose a point on the wall to begin fixing them to achieve a symmetrical appearance.

Because there are so many designs of tile from which to choose, and a variety of ways in which they can be used, you must have a clear idea of what you will do before you start work. The best method is to sketch out a paper plan. In fact, a paper plan is essential for calculating how many tiles to buy; and you can use a similar drawing to decide where to put dados, borders, inset tiles, picture panels and so on.

Once you know what to use and how, start work on the wall itself by marking out the horizontal and vertical starting lines and nailing battens to the wall to support the tiles.

This chapter contains

Planning

Once you have decided on the types of tile you want to use, you need to work out just how many you will require. The first task is to determine the area to be tiled, whether it is a simple splashback or a complete room. The easiest way of doing this is to draw up a plan, mark all the relevant dimensions on it and calculate the area from them. Tiles are sold in various quantities in packs, boxes and cartons, and your supplier will be able to advise you on the quantity needed.

Remember to allow extra for cutting in at the edges and for breakages. For an area of 5sq m (5sq yd), buy ten per cent more than you need; for a larger area, add an extra five per cent. Work out the tiling pattern: where you will place inset tiles or feature panels, and whether you will want a dado or border tiles. With the latter, you need to know the total length required, rather than the area.

DRAWING A PAPER PLAN

Draw a plan of the wall, or portion of wall, to be tiled. If you are tiling a whole room, draw each wall separately. There is no need to make the drawings accurate in terms of scale, simply use them as a visual guide to the important features that must be included in your calculations. However, the dimensions you mark on them must be taken from accurate measurements. You can use either metric or imperial units of measurement. Use these dimensions to calculate the actual area to be tiled. If you are unsure of this process, take the plan to your tile supplier who will be able to make the calculations for you.

For a whole room, draw up a plan like this, marking on it the dimensions of the walls, windows, doors and other features that must be considered.

For each feature, multiply the length by the height to calculate its area, adding all the resulting figures together. Subtract this figure from the total wall area to obtain the area that needs tiling.

From this, you can work out the quantity of tiles to buy, plus the amount of adhesive and grout.

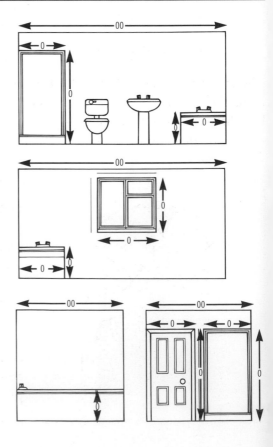

TILING PATTERNS

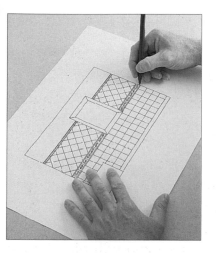

Although tiles are commonly fixed in line both horizontally and vertically, they can also be arranged in diagonal rows or in brick fashion to provide additional interest. Particularly attractive schemes can be devised by combining these arrangements in bands separated by patterned or contrasting dado tiles.

To work out the most effective pattern, use a large sheet of paper to draw up another plan of the walls, as this will allow plenty of room to fill in all the details. Having drawn in the relevant features, add the positions of patterned tiles, insets, dados, etc. Or use it to decide on the kind of tiling arrangement you would like. If you photocopy the original drawings of the walls, you can try several arrangements to see which you prefer.

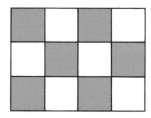

The conventional method of fixing tiles is to align the rows both horizontally and vertically, to give continuous horizontal and vertical joints.

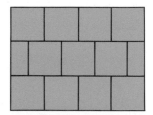

For additional interest, the tiles in each row can be staggered in relation to their neighbours, brick fashion. This works particularly well with oblong tiles.

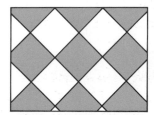

Another attractive pattern is achieved by fixing the rows of tiles diagonally to create a diamond pattern. This works best with square tiles.

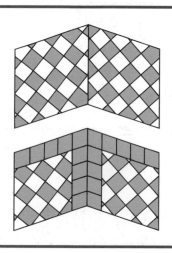

COPING WITH CORNERS

If you intend arranging the tiles in a particular pattern, or are using patterned tiles, and you are tiling adjacent walls, continuing the pattern from one wall on to another may be quite difficult (top), the more so if the corners of the room are not truly vertical. In some situations, this may be completely impossible.

A simple solution to this problem is to edge the patterned area of tiles with plain tiles fixed in conventional vertical and horizontal rows. This has the effect of producing patterned panels (bottom).

Setting out

Having purchased the tiles, and with the wall prepared for tiling, you can begin setting out. This task is essential to determine the point at which you should fix the first tile, to ensure that the overall arrangement is symmetrical.

You must support the tiles while the adhesive dries, otherwise they will slide down the wall. To do this, temporarily nail a horizontal wooden batten near the base of the wall. You cannot rely on the skirting board or floor for support, as neither is likely to be perfectly level.

TOOLS: Tape measure, pencil, spirit level, long straight-edged batten, gauge rod, hammer

MATERIALS: Two 50 x 25mm (2 x 1in) straight softwood battens, masonry nails

MAKING A GAUGE ROD

1 To make a gauge rod, lay out a row of tiles with tile spacers between them. Place the batten alongside, one end level with the edge of the first tile. Mark the tile positions on it, allowing for the gaps in between. With hand-made tiles, which are irregular in size, allow a spacing of 5–8mm (³⁄16– ⁵⁄16in).

A gauge rod is an essential tool when tiling any large area, and is easily made from a wooden batten about 1.8m (6ft) long (or shorter if you are only tiling a short wall). It allows you to determine where the horizontal and vertical rows of tiles will fall on the wall, so that you can see whether tiles need to be cut at the ends of the rows and, if so, by how much. Using the rod, you can also determine the positions of the supporting battens.

2 For clarity, extend the pencil marks across the face of the rod, making sure that they are square to the edge. You can do this with the aid of another tile. If you wish, you can number the divisions on the rod so that you can see at a glance how many tiles there will be in each row.

SETTING OUT

1 Measure the length of the wall to be tiled and make a pencil mark at the centre. Then, holding the straight-edged batten vertically, with the aid of a spirit level, draw a vertical line from floor to ceiling at the point of the mark.

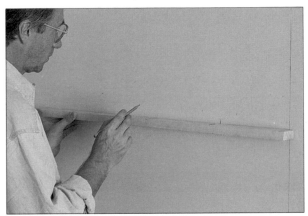

2 Hold the mark at the end of the gauge rod against the line on the wall to determine where the vertical rows of tiles will fall. On a long run, it may help to mark off the tile positions on the wall.

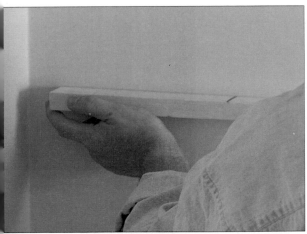

3 At the end of the wall, the gauge rod will show you whether a cut tile will be required and, if so, its width. Because you began from the centre of the wall, the same width of tile will be needed at the other end of the wall. If you are left with a very narrow gap to fill, you may have difficulty in cutting a sliver of tile to fit, and if the corner is uneven you may run into serious problems with the sliver tapering to nothing.

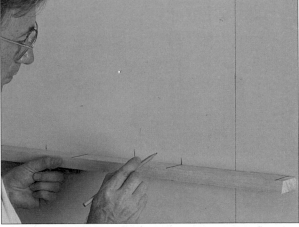

4 It will look much better if any cut tiles are at least half a tile wide. So go back to your centre line, and hold the gauge rod so that the end mark on it is offset to one side of the centre line by half a tile's width. Then make a mark on the wall in line with the end mark. Draw a new vertical line at this point, which will now be your starting point. In this way, the actual centre line of the wall will pass through the centre of a tile.

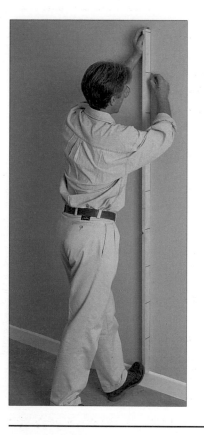

5 Next, determine the positions of the horizontal rows of tiles. First hold the gauge rod against your vertical starting line with one end touching the skirting or floor, as appropriate. Then make a pencil mark on the wall so that it is level with the topmost mark on the gauge rod.

6 Hold the end of the rod against the ceiling and check if any mark on it aligns with the wall mark. If it does, you will not need to cut tiles for the top and bottom rows. If not, look at the gap between the wall mark and the nearest mark on the rod below it; halving this distance gives the depth of cut tiles at top and bottom. If these are very narrow, mark the wall level with the next mark down on the rod. Remember that ceilings are rarely perfectly level and often necessitate some cutting.

7 Measure the distance between the two pencil marks on the wall. Then make a third pencil mark exactly midway between these two points. This will give you an idea of the depth of cut tiles needed top and bottom.

8 Holding the gauge rod so that one end is just clear of the skirting, and with one of its marks aligned with the third wall mark, make another mark on the wall at the foot of the rod. This represents your starting point for the first horizontal row of tiles and ensures that the cut tiles at top and bottom will be equal in depth.

COPING WITH OBSTRUCTIONS

Windows, doors and other fixtures can complicate setting out a wall for tiling, particularly if they are towards one end of the wall. The important point to remember is to work from the centre of the most prominent visual feature when setting out, but be prepared to amend the starting point if you run into problems with very narrow cut tiles at the ends of the walls, or at windows or doors. Take your time when faced with this situation, using the gauge rod to determine the ideal starting point.

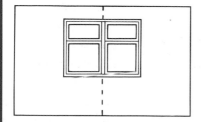
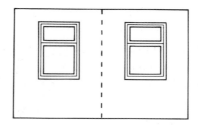
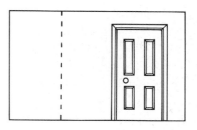

Where the wall contains a single window, placed near the centre, use the centre line of the window as your starting point when setting out with the gauge rod.

On a wall containing two windows, it is better to work from the centre line of the section of wall between the windows, as this will give a much more balanced look to the tiling.

If the window or door is offset at one end of the wall, work from the centre line of the section of wall between the furthest corner and the door or window frame.

9 Nail a horizontal wooden batten to the wall in line with the pencil mark, using a spirit level to ensure that it is perfectly level. Do not drive the nails all the way in; leave their heads protruding so that you can remove the batten easily.

10 When you begin tiling, work outwards from the vertical starting line. You can simply align the tiles with this line, but it will be easier with a definite edge to work from, so nail a vertical batten to the wall in line with the pencil line.

Tiling a Wall

Cladding a large area with tiles, such as a complete wall, is quite an ambitious undertaking, but if you take care and have prepared the surface correctly, the result will be very rewarding.

Although you need to work quite quickly, particularly when applying grout, don't rush the job, as you may make irretrievable mistakes. Assemble your tiles, adhesive and tools and have any paper plan to hand so that you can place patterned or inset tiles exactly where they are required. Tile a small area at a time, making sure the tiles are spaced correctly and bedded properly so that they are all level.

A tile that is lower than, or stands proud of, its neighbours will ruin the appearance of a tiled surface. Deal with that problem while you are fixing the tiles, not afterwards when the adhesive has set.

Field tiles

When tiling a large area, you begin by filling in the central portion with whole tiles, working outwards from the centre and upwards from the bottom. These tiles are known as the field tiles. They are set in a bed of adhesive spread on the wall with a notched spreader that leaves ridges of adhesive rather than a continuous layer.

To ensure uniform gaps between tiles, you can fit plastic cross-shaped spacers between them, or alternatively use pieces of card or matchsticks. Work on a small area at a time, otherwise you may find the adhesive beginning to harden before you have finished.

TOOLS: Small trowel, notched adhesive spreader, sponge, bucket

MATERIALS: Tiles, tile adhesive, tile spacers, water

1 As tile adhesive begins to harden once exposed to the air, it is best to work on an area no greater than 1sq m (1sq yd) at a time. Use a small trowel to scoop some adhesive on to the wall, then spread it out horizontally with the notched spreader. Make sure that the teeth of the spreader actually touch the wall's surface so that you are left with a series of parallel strips of adhesive, as shown. Work away from the vertical guide batten.

2 Place the first tile in position so that it sits on the horizontal batten and is hard up against the vertical batten. Press it firmly against the wall.

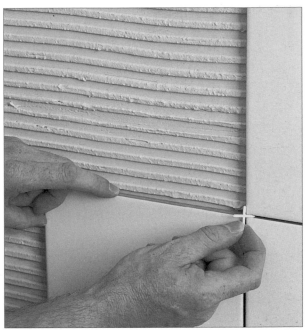

3 Add the next horizontal tile and the first tile of the row above, bedding them firmly in the adhesive by wiggling them slightly while pressing firmly with your hand. Space them initially by eye.

4 Fit tile spacers to ensure even gaps for grouting. The adhesive is flexible enough to allow you to move the tiles slightly. Hand-made tiles need larger gaps, so use cardboard or offcuts of wood as spacers.

5 Carry on until you have tiled the area of adhesive. Then wipe over the faces of the tiles with a damp sponge to remove any splashes of adhesive. This is essential; if you wait until the job is finished, the adhesive will have hardened and be very difficult to remove. Carry on in this manner until all the field tiles have been stuck to the wall.

MIXING TILES

Coloured tiles or tiles with coloured patterns may vary slightly in shade from batch to batch. Using tiles from one box at a time may result in distinct colour changes across the surface. However, any variations in shade will be far less noticeable if you mix tiles from different boxes before you begin work.

Fixing uneven tiles

When tiling a wall, your aim should be to produce a perfectly flat surface, and if you have prepared the wall properly, this should not be too difficult. Any slight undulations in the wall surface can be accommodated by varying the thickness of adhesive slightly.

If you don't make the effort to level the faces of the tiles, the appearance of the finished job will be ruined: any light falling on the tiles will pick out high and low areas by casting tell-tale shadows. So you should check constantly for low or high tiles, and if you find any, remove them and bed them on fresh adhesive so that they match their neighbours.

TOOLS: Spirit level/wooden straight edge, filling knife, notched adhesive spreader, claw hammer

MATERIALS: Tile adhesive

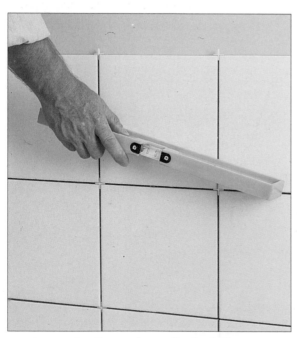

1 As you fix tiles to the wall, check from time to time that they are level by holding a straight edge, such as a spirit level or wooden batten, across them. This will show up any that are lower or higher than the rest.

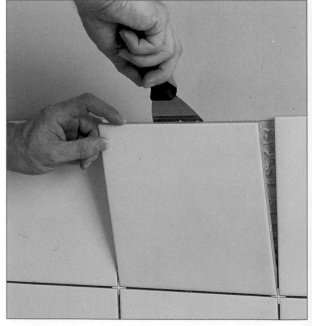

2 If you find a tile that is too low or too high, lever it from the wall carefully, using a flat-bladed tool. Take care not to dislodge or damage any of the surrounding tiles, particularly if the tile being removed is in the centre of a tiled area.

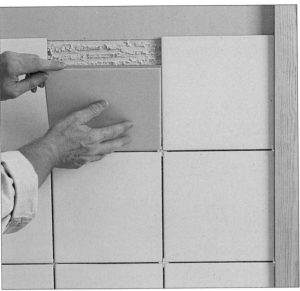

3 Scrape the adhesive from the back of the tile and spread on a fresh layer, using the notched spreader. If the tile was low, you can add a little more adhesive than normal; if high, a little less.

4 Press the tile back on to the wall, bedding it firmly and replacing any spacers to set the grouting gap. Make a final check with the straight edge that the tile is now level with its neighbours.

REMOVING THE BATTENS

1 Once you have tiled from the vertical batten to one end of the wall, you can remove the batten and work in the other direction. Then, when you have completed the wall above the horizontal batten, leave the adhesive to set before removing it. Finally, fill in between the lowest row of tiles and the skirting or floor.

Use a claw hammer to prise out the nails so that you can remove the battens. Take care not to dislodge any of the tiles that butt up against them.

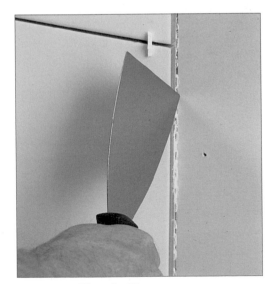

2 Use a filling knife to scrape away any adhesive that has oozed between the tiles and batten, as this may prevent you from obtaining the correct spacing between these and the subsequent tiles.

Inserting edge tiles

Unless you are extremely lucky and have a wall that is an exact number of whole tiles long and an exact number of whole tiles high, you will need to cut some tiles to fill gaps at the ends and at the top and bottom of the wall. This is not as difficult as it might first seem, and the variety of cutting tools available – if used properly – will ensure accurate cuts every time.

Accuracy is the watchword, however. Take careful measurements of the gaps that need filling, and measure for each tile that needs cutting: don't assume that all the tiles needed to fill a gap along, say, one end of a wall will be the same size, as the corners of rooms – whether between walls or between a wall and a ceiling or floor – rarely run true.

TOOLS: Tape measure, felt-tip pen/chinagraph pencil, steel rule, tile spike, tile file, notched adhesive spreader

MATERIALS: Tiles, tile adhesive, tile spacers

1 Take measurements at the top and bottom of the gap (or each end, if you are filling-in at the ceiling or floor). If the tiled area is to end at the adjacent wall, allow a gap for grouting; if the tiling is to continue on that wall, the cut tile need not fit exactly into the corner, as the tile on the adjacent wall will hide any gap.

2 Transfer the measurements to a tile with a felt-tip pen or chinagraph pencil, remembering that the cut edge is the one that should fit into the corner. Then use a steel rule and a tile spike to score the glaze between the two marks. Press firmly with the spike and score the tile once only in one smooth movement.

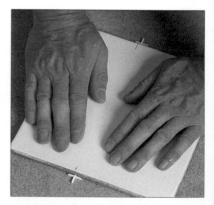

3 Place the tile on a firm surface with one leg of a tile spacer under each end of the scored line. Then press down firmly on both sides of the line and the tile should snap cleanly in two. If it does not, you probably have not scored it well enough, or the spacers may be out of line.

4 After cutting, clean up any roughness on the edge of the tile with a tile file, holding it at right angles to the edge.

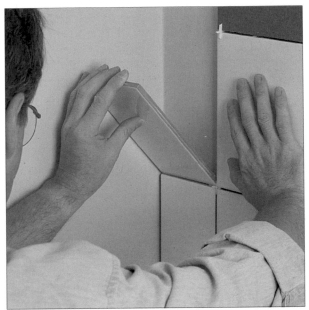

5 Place the cut piece of tile in the gap to check whether it fits securely. If necessary, make any adjustments to its shape by filing.

6 When you are happy with the fit, spread a layer of adhesive on the back of the cut tile, using the end of the notched spreader.

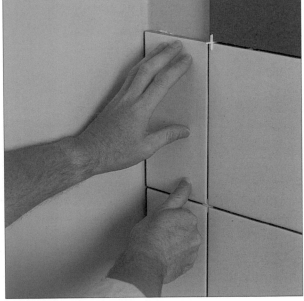

7 Press the tile firmly into place, wiggling it slightly to bed it and adjusting its position so that you can insert spacers at the top and bottom.

Methods of cutting

The tile spike is the simplest and least expensive tool for cutting tiles (see page 42), and for a small job it is probably not worth investing in anything more complex. However, there are several more sophisticated tools available that make cutting tiles much easier. If you expect to be cutting a lot of tiles, or if the tiles you are using are particularly hard, it will be worth investing in one of these.

NIBBLERS

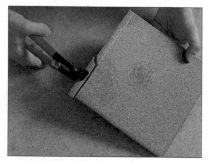

If you only have a narrow sliver to remove from a tile, or want to remove the waste from a cut-out, nibblers are essential. With these you grip a small portion of tile, then break it off by levering the tool downwards.

To remove a narrow strip from the edge of a tile, score the glaze with a tile spike. Then hold the tile firmly in one hand while gripping a portion of the waste with the nibbler jaws, close to the scored line. Lever downwards with the nibblers and a piece of waste will break away along the line. Remove the rest of the waste in the same way.

COMBINED CUTTING WHEEL/SNAPPER

This simple hand tool combines a cutting wheel for scoring the glaze of a tile with a pair of angled jaws that can be used to snap it along the scored line. It is ideal for cutting small tiles or tiles with heavily studded backs.

1 Measure the gap to be filled and mark the tile as normal. Then, using a steel rule as a guide, run the wheel over the tile between the two marks to score it. Push down firmly and score the tile only once.

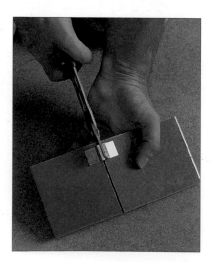

2 Place the tile in the jaws of the tool, aligning the scored line carefully with the centre of the angled jaws. Squeeze the handles together and the tile will snap cleanly along the scored line; surprisingly little pressure is required. Be careful not to let the pieces drop, as they may shatter if they hit a hard surface.

TILE-CUTTING MACHINE

If you expect to be cutting a lot of tiles, particularly if they are large and/or very hard, it will be worth investing in a tile-cutting machine. Alternatively, you should be able to hire a professional-quality machine from a tool hire shop. Several different types of machine are available, some offering more facilities than others. All, however, combine a scoring function with a snapping action that requires very little pressure.

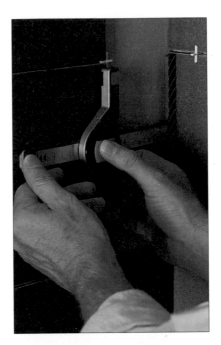

1 Some machines are provided with a removable gauge that allows you to measure the gap to be filled. This particular version makes an allowance for the grouting gap, and it can also be adjusted to measure a tapering space. Fit it so that the end of the gauge is resting firmly against the adjacent wall or tiled surface, and the tabs of the sliding portion against the edge of the neighbouring tile. A simple over-centre lever can then be used to lock the gauge in this position, allowing it to be transferred to the machine.

2 Having locked the sliding portion of the gauge in place, fit the assembly into its cut-out in the bed of the machine. Take care not to disturb the gauge setting while you are doing this, otherwise the tile will be cut to the incorrect size.

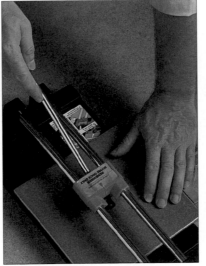

3 Place the tile in the machine, aligning one edge with the tabs of the gauge and the other with the stops moulded into the bed. Bring the scriber into contact with the tile, press down firmly and push the handle forwards to score the glaze.

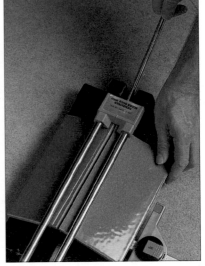

4 Set the tile under the handle slide so that the scored line on the tile is aligned with the mark on the slide. Then lower the handle to bring the snapper into contact with the underside of the tile. Press down and the tile will snap in two.

Grouting

Once you have fixed all the tiles to the wall, the adhesive should be allowed to dry before the gaps between the tiles are grouted. The amount of time for the adhesive to dry will vary depending on the type of adhesive used: see the manufacturer's instructions.

Some grouts are supplied in powder form for mixing with water, while others come ready-mixed. Make sure you have sufficient to complete the tiled area, and be prepared to work quickly, as it will begin to harden and become unworkable quite quickly. Make sure you use a waterproof version for a shower cubicle. Before applying the grout, either remove cross-shaped tile spacers or push them in as far as they will go.

TOOLS: Small trowel, grout spreader/squeegee, grout shaper, sponge, bucket, soft clean cloth

MATERIALS: Grout, water

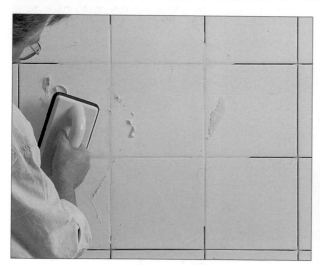

1 Use the trowel to scoop up some grout and press it on to the face of the tiles. Then spread the grout with the squeegee, wiping it from the face of the tiles and pressing it into the open joints between them. Use a smooth, diagonal, sweeping action, working up and across the tiles. Work quickly until you have grouted all the joints.

2 Carefully go over the tiled area with a damp sponge to remove all traces of grout from the surface of the tiles. Do this as soon as you finish applying the grout, as it will be very difficult to remove once it has been allowed to harden. Take care not to drag any grout from the joints while you are doing this.

GROUT SHAPERS

You can either buy a special tool for shaping grout or make your own. Some ready-made grout shapers offer a choice of profile size and have interchangeable heads so that when one becomes worn, another can be fitted in its place.

Alternatively, you can use a large-diameter wooden dowel with the end neatly and smoothly rounded off, or even the tip of an old plastic paintbrush handle. If you do choose either of these home-made tools, experiment on a small area of tiling first in case the material discolours the grout.

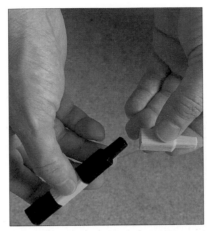

1 This proprietary grout shaper features four interchangeable sections that offer a choice of shaping profiles. They also allow a fresh profile to be selected when the one in use becomes too worn to be effective.

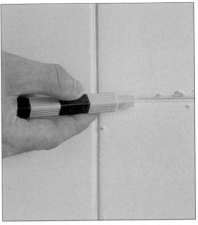

2 Shape the grout after it has hardened slightly, holding the tool so that it runs along the edges of the adjacent tiles, the corner of the tip smoothing the grout. Sponge off any grout squeezed out at the sides.

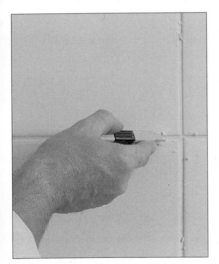

3 Allow the grout to harden slightly, then shape the joints to give a uniform appearance. Pull the shaper along each vertical and horizontal joint in one continuous movement. Remove any surplus grout with a sponge.

4 If the shaping process exposes any gaps or holes in the grouted joints, press a small amount of fresh grout into them with your fingertip. Then shape the joint as before and remove any surplus.

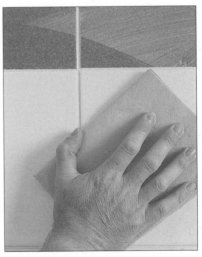

5 Leave the grout to harden fully. As the sponged face of the tiles dries, you will notice a powdery residue covering the surface. This should be polished off with a soft, clean cloth to leave a perfect finish.

Borders and Dados

Although there are many excellent patterned tiles to choose from, you may feel that using them, particularly to tile a complete wall, would produce too busy an appearance for your taste. Even if you only want to tile a small splashback, plain tiles may be preferable. However, an area of plain tiles can look a little bland, and a large area cold and uninteresting. Adding some form of pattern or contrasting colour will provide a focus for the eye and sufficient visual interest without becoming overwhelming.

The simple way to do this is to add a border of contrasting tiles to splashbacks and half-tiled walls, or a dado course to a completely tiled wall. Special narrow border and dado tiles are made just for this purpose, although you can also use contrasting coloured or patterned standard tiles in the same manner if you prefer.

Another advantage of using dado tiles is that they can be used to provide a break between different coloured or patterned tiles, or between tiling patterns, on the same wall.

Border tiles

If you are tiling a small area of wall such as a splashback, or are half-tiling a wall, you may want to finish off the edge with a contrasting or decorative border. Indeed, you may have no option if the tiles you are using have no glazed edges. The simplest way of doing this is to use a standard tile in a contrasting colour or with a pattern of some sort. Alternatively, you can use tile trim or a wooden moulding.

However, on a basin splashback, normal sized tiles may be too large, dominating the central portion of the tiled area. In this situation, it would be better to use a proprietary border tile. These are much narrower than standard tiles and come in variety of colours and patterns. Although you may be able to find border tiles that match the size of your field tiles, it is quite possible that they won't. In this case, you must stagger their joints in relation to the joints between the field tiles.

TOOLS: Tape measure, felt-tip pen/chinagraph pencil, steel rule, tile spike, tile file, small trowel, notched adhesive spreader, sponge, bucket

MATERIALS: Standard or border tiles, tile adhesive, tile spacers, water

STANDARD SIZE TILES

The simplest method of adding a border to a splashback or similar area of tiles is to use tiles of the same size as the field tiles, but in a contrasting colour or pattern. This can be quite effective, but take care not to allow the border to overpower the scheme, which it could do on a small area of tiles.

When half-tiling a wall, you should ensure that the top row of tiles are whole tiles, not cut tiles. This will look better, whether you are using a contrasting border or not.

CHANGING DIRECTION

When fixing border tiles around a splashback, you may find that you need to change the direction of the tiles from horizontal to vertical. If the tiles are a plain colour, there will be no problems; you can simply overlap the end of one tile with another. However, if they are patterned, this method will not produce a very neat corner, as the pattern will not match. Fortunately, there are two possible solutions.

1 Depending on the pattern, it may be possible to mitre the ends of the adjacent tiles so that the design continues from the horizontal row onto the vertical row without an apparent break. You may need to trim the tiles carefully to obtain a good match. Cut both before fixing them to the wall.

2 When the tiles have been grouted, the mitred joint will look neat and unobtrusive. Note how the joints of the border tiles have been staggered in relation to those of the field tiles. This is necessary because of their different sizes. The size variation between the tiles is quite common.

3 In some cases, the pattern may be impossible to match up by mitring the ends of the tiles. In this situation, the answer is to fill the corner with a small square of plain tile, which can be cut easily from a larger one.

4 Here the square of tile has been cut from one of the coloured field tiles, but a plain white tile would have worked as well. Make sure you use a tile with glazed edges, cutting the square from a corner to provide two glazed sides.

Dados

A dado is a useful means of breaking up a large expanse of tiles, such as a whole wall. It runs around the wall at waist height, and is ideal as a division between different coloured or patterned tiles, or between different tiling patterns, or simply to provide interest on an otherwise plain wall.

As with borders, contrasting or patterned standard tiles can be used to form a simple dado, which makes setting out easy. Alternatively, a wooden dado rail could be used. However, purpose-made dado tiles offer the greatest flexibility in terms of width, colour and pattern, and many have moulded relief patterns which provide even greater interest to a tiled area.

TOOLS: Tape measure, felt-tip pen/chinagraph pencil, tile saw, small trowel, notched adhesive spreader, sponge, bucket

MATERIALS: Dado tiles, tile adhesive, tile spacers, water

CUTTING MOULDED TILES

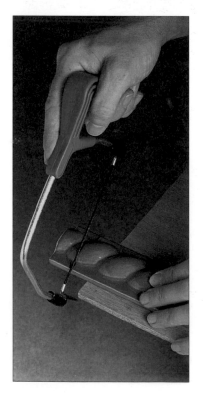

Dado tiles with a moulded relief pattern are impossible to score and snap in the conventional manner when cutting them to length. The solution is to cut them with a tile saw. Mark the tile for length with a felt-tip pen or chinagraph pencil, then cut along the line with the tile saw.

CONCEALING THE END

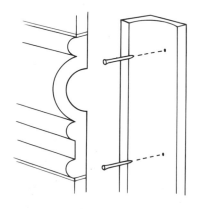

Dados do not have to be used solely for breaking up large expanses of tiles. They are equally effective when set in splashbacks, either in the bathroom or kitchen. Some, however, are formed into shapes that would leave unsightly openings at the edge of the splashback. These need concealing, and the simplest way of doing so is with a length of decorative wooden moulding.

Pin the moulding along the edge of the splashback with masonry nails. Using a punch, drive the nails below the surface of the wood, fill the resulting holes and either stain or paint the moulding.

◀ Here a patterned dado tile makes an effective break between a lower panel of subtly coloured tiles, fixed in a conventional pattern, from a panel of white tiles fixed diagonally. A small insert echoes the dado pattern and makes an effective accent on the white background.

▲ To break up an expanse of white tiles, this dado has been created from three separate tiles. The central tile, with its relief pattern picked out in olive green, is flanked by a narrow dado moulding at the top and a pencil moulding at the bottom, both in the same colour.

◀ This diamond-pattern marble dado strip is provided on a mesh backing, much like mosaic tiles. Notice how a solid row of dark tiles has been used above and below the dado to emphasise it.

Tiling Awkward Areas

When tiling a large area such as a complete wall, or even a complete room, you will inevitably run into situations where you need to fit the tiles around corners or awkwardly shaped objects such as pipes, electrical outlets and bathroom fittings.

In some cases, where the item concerned is surface-mounted, it may be better to remove it from the wall, fix the tiles and then refit it, drilling holes through the tiles for the fixing screws. This can often be neater than cutting tiles around it. However, this may not always be possible or desirable, in which case the tiles must be cut and fixed accordingly.

Coping with corners is a relatively straightforward process, but cutting tiles to fit around odd-shaped items requires care. It is not difficult to do, provided you use the correct techniques and take your time.

Corners

The most common problem when tiling walls is dealing with corners. You may have to cope with an external corner (one that projects outwards), an internal corner, or both; a different method is used in each case to ensure a neat finish.

The important consideration is that the horizontal rows of tiles on the adjacent surfaces must align. You must take care when setting out to ensure that the support battens are perfectly aligned with each other, as any misalignment will be immediately noticeable and will spoil the finished tiling. Check also that an external angle is truly vertical with a spirit level. If it is not, the ends of the tiles will need to overlap it slightly, tile trim being used to finish off the corner neatly.

TOOLS: Tape measure, pencil, spirit level, hacksaw, small trowel, notched adhesive spreader, sponge, bucket

MATERIALS: Tiles, tile adhesive, corner trim, tile spacers, water

INTERNAL CORNERS

At an internal corner, the tiles on one wall are fixed so that they overlap the ends of the tiles on the adjacent wall. The result should be a neat grouted joint in the angle between the two walls.

You will probably have to cut tiles to fit into the corner on both walls, but if you can fix uncut tiles on one wall, for neatness use them to conceal the cut edges of the others.

Tile one wall completely first, cutting the edge tiles into the angle between the two walls. They do not have to be an exact fit since the overlapping tiles will hide any slight gap between them and the facing wall. When tiling the neighbouring wall, take accurate measurements for each edge tile, allowing for the grouting between it and the existing tiled wall. Then fix the tiles in place to complete the corner.

EXTERNAL CORNERS

At an external corner, the simplest solution is to use plastic corner trim to hide the edges of the tiles and provide a neat finish to the angle between the adjacent walls. The trim has a quadrant profile with a perforated mounting flange for bedding in the tile adhesive. They are available in a range of colours, to suit different thicknesses of tile.

1 Tile one of the walls completely, so that the edges of the tiles are flush with the end of the wall. Cut the corner trim to length with a hacksaw, then apply a narrow band of tile adhesive to the face of the other wall (called the return wall) from top to bottom. Carefully press the trim into the adhesive, aligning it with the edges of the tiles on the adjacent wall. Remember to insert tile spacers between the trim and edges of the tiles.

2 Spread more adhesive on the second (return) wall, working the spreader vertically, rather than horizontally. This will prevent the spreader from catching the trim and pulling it from the corner.

3 Tile the return wall, working away from the corner trim. Place the tiles so that they almost touch the trim, then fit tile spacers between the trim and the tiles to ensure an even grouted joint. Grout the joints as normal when the adhesive has set.

GLAZED-EDGE TILES

If you are using tiles with bevelled or rounded glazed edges, you can tackle external corners without the need for corner trim, provided the corner is truly vertical. Simply fix the tiles on one wall so that they overlap the edges of the tiles on the other.

Tile the return wall so that the tiles are flush with the face of the main wall. Then fix the glazed-edge tiles on the main wall so that they overlap and conceal the edges of the tiles on the return wall.

Window recesses

Tiling a window recess produces its own particular problems, as it has effectively an external corner all the way round, requiring the corner trim to be joined at the ends. In addition, the reveal is likely to be quite narrow and will involve cutting tiles to fit in. You will also need to find some means of holding tiles in place at the top of the recess while the adhesive sets.

The procedure is to first tile the face of the wall surrounding the window recess, then the underside of the reveal, the sides, and finally the bottom.

TOOLS: Tape measure, pencil, small trowel, notched adhesive spreader, tile spike, steel rule, hacksaw, hammer

MATERIALS: Tiles, tile adhesive, corner trim, wooden battens, masonry nails

1 Begin by tiling the face of the wall up to the window recess so that the edges of the tiles are flush with the reveal. Cut lengths of corner trim to fit around the recess, mitring the ends so that they fit neatly together.

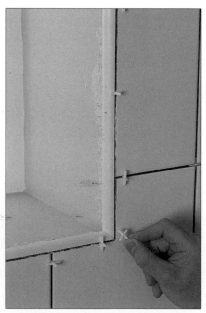

2 If you don't have a mitre block, measure back along one side of the trim a distance equal to its width. Join this point with the opposite corner and saw off the triangular piece of waste. Fit spacers when fixing the trim.

3 When tiling the reveal itself, fix whole tiles around the outer edge of the reveal so that they butt up to the corner trim. Then fill in the remaining space against the window frame with cut tiles.

SUPPORTING THE TILES

The main problem when tiling a window recess completely is holding the tiles in place at the top of the recess while the adhesive sets. This applies to both the tiles on the face of the wall and on the underside of the reveal. The simplest method is to use wooden battens for temporary support while the tile and adhesive sets.

▲ To support the tiles on the face of the wall, temporarily nail a wooden batten in place so that its upper edge is level with the underside of the reveal. When the tiles have been fixed in place and the adhesive has set completely, remove the batten and finish tiling the face of the wall where the batten was nailed.

◀ To support the tiles on the underside of the reveal while the adhesive sets, use a wooden batten wedged in place with two uprights.

OVERLAPPING EDGES

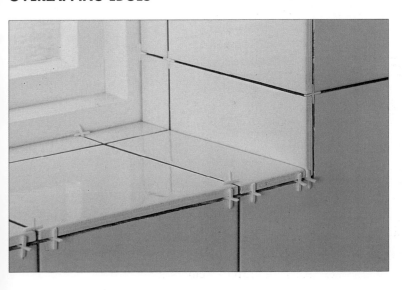

Tiles with glazed edges can be used to finish around a window recess without the need for corner trim, as with external corners. One set of tiles – those on the horizontal window sill – simply overlap the edges of those on the adjacent vertical surface.

As with corner trim, fix tiles to the face of the wall so that their top edges are flush with the reveal. Then fix whole tiles in place around the recess so that they overlap the edges of the tiles on the face of the wall.

Pipes

Some rooms that need tiling have pipes that either pass through the wall or run along its face. Ideally, these should be concealed by boxing them in. If, however, boxing is not feasible, you may have to cut a tile to fit around a pipe, or drill the face of the tiles for pipe clips. Neither task is particularly difficult, but when cutting around a pipe, you must measure and mark out your tile with care if it is to fit accurately.

You can use the same technique for tiling around an electrical outlet or switch, but for this, turn off the power to the circuit, remove the faceplate, tile up to the edge of the box behind, then replace the faceplate.

TOOLS: Pencil, felt-tip pen/chinagraph pencil, steel rule, tile spike, narrow nibblers, tile file, hammer, electric drill, masonry/tile bit, screwdriver

MATERIALS: Tiles, tile adhesive, pipe offcut, masking tape, masonry nail, wall plugs, screws, pipe clips

CUTTING AROUND A PIPE

If only one tile will be affected when cutting around a pipe, the technique is to split the tile on the centre line of the pipe and make a semi-circular cut-out in each piece to fit around the pipe. If the position of the pipe coincides with a joint between tiles, this procedure will have to be adapted to suit.

2 Next, transfer the pencil marks to the tile that will be cut around the pipe, using a felt-tip pen or chinagraph pencil. Remember to place tile spacers in position so that the marks will be in the correct position on the tile.

1 Having tiled the wall to one side and below the pipe, use a tile and a pencil to mark lines on the wall level with the top, bottom and sides of the pipe where it projects from the wall.

3 Using another tile as a guide to ensure that the lines are at right-angles to the edges of the tile, extend the marks across the face with your felt-tip pen or chinagraph pencil. Where the pairs of lines intersect, carefully draw around an offcut of pipe of the correct diameter to mark out the area to be removed.

PIPE CLIPS

If you want to run a pipe across the face of a tiled surface, you will have to drill the tiles for fixing screws and fit pipe clips. The same technique can be used for fixing any surface-mounted fitting, such as a mirror, toilet roll holder or soap dish, to a tiled surface.

1 Cover the area of the tile to be drilled with masking tape. This will allow you to mark the hole positions with a pencil and help prevent the drill bit from skidding – particularly if you are using a masonry bit. You can make doubly sure of drilling accurately by using a masonry nail to break the glaze at the point to be drilled. A light tap on the nail with a hammer should be all that is necessary.
Drill holes for the screws, using a bit that matches the size of the wall plugs to be used.

2 Having drilled the holes to the correct depth, remove the masking tape from the face of the tile and fit plastic wall plugs in the holes. Finally, offer up the pipe and clip, securing the latter to the wall by driving the screws into the plastic plugs.

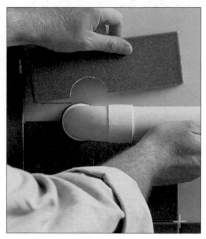

4 Score across the face of the tile so that the scored line passes through the centre of the circle. Whether you score the line vertically or horizontally will depend on the way the pipe runs; use the pipe itself to conceal as much of the cut as possible. Then snap the tile in two.

5 Using narrow nibblers, carefully remove the waste from within each semi-circle. When you get close to the line, offer up the tile to check its fit. Having removed enough waste, carefully smooth the edges with a tile file. Then clean the face of the tile to remove the pen marks.

6 Make a final check before fixing the pieces of tile to the wall. Then spread adhesive on them and stick them in place. If you scored the tile correctly, the joint between the two pieces should be almost invisible. Fill any slight gap around the pipe when you grout the tiles.

Bathroom fittings

There may be occasions when you need to tile around an item with a large, irregular shape, such as a washbasin or a similar fitting in a bathroom. In this situation, the ideal solution is to pull the item away from the wall as much as possible and tile behind it, even if this involves modifying any pipework slightly: the end result will certainly be much neater. If this is not possible, you will need to make cut-outs in the tiles surrounding the item so that they fit neatly against it.

TOOLS: Scissors, felt-tip pen/chinagraph pencil, tile spike, steel rule, nibblers, tile file, profile gauge, spirit level, tape measure

MATERIALS: Tiles, paper, self-adhesive tape

IDEAL TOOLS

Tile saw

Although nibblers can be used to make cut-outs in tiles, you may find that a tile saw is easier to use. This looks like a small hacksaw, but it has a special blade that will cut through ceramic tiles with ease. Having marked the area to be cut out of the tile, hold it firmly and simply saw along the outline. Because the blade is round, you can change direction quite easily and cut quite tight curves.

Profile gauge

A profile gauge is useful for transferring an unusual shape to a tile. It incorporates a large number of sliding plastic 'needles'  which duplicate the shape of an item as the tool is pushed against it. The gauge is ideal for use with small tiles, but for larger tiles you may have to find some way of supporting it in the correct position to cover the required area of the tile.

1 The simplest method for transferring the shape of the basin to the tile is to make a paper template. First, cut a piece of paper to the size of the tile, then make scissor cuts in the paper so that you have a series of paper 'fingers'. The direction in which you make the cuts will depend on the cut-out's position. In this case, the shape will be in the corner of the tile, so cuts are made in both directions.

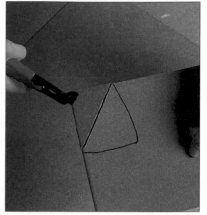

2 With tile spacers in place between the adjacent tiles, hold the paper in position as if it was a tile. Smooth the paper against the wall and fold the paper fingers back where they meet the basin.

3 Tape the fingers down to prevent them from moving about, then lay the paper template on top of the tile to be cut. Mark the outline of the cutout on the tile with a felt-tip pen or chinagraph pencil.

4 In this case, a large portion of the waste can be removed by simply scoring a line diagonally across it with a tile spike, then snapping it off with a pair of nibblers. This will save you time.

5 The remaining waste must be removed with nibblers. Don't try to snap off too much at once; take your time and break off small pieces, working towards the outline. As you get close to the line, take even smaller 'bites', until eventually you are almost scraping off slivers of tile.

6 Clean up the edge of the tile with a tile file, then hold the tile against the wall to check the fit around the basin. If necessary, adjust the fit with the nibblers and tile file. When you are happy that you have a uniform gap around the basin, you can fix the tile to the wall.

7 Continue to cut and fit tiles around the rest of the washbasin in the same manner. When you have finished, you can tile the remainder of the wall as normal. The gap around the washbasin should be grouted when you grout the tiles to leave a neat finish.

Splashbacks and Worktops

Tiles can also be used in smaller areas, as a practical panel rather than as a main part of the decor. A splashback behind a handbasin, around a bath or along the back of a kitchen worktop, for example, will protect the wall and can provide an attractive decorative feature at the same time.

The techniques for attaching the tiles to the wall are essentially the same as for tiling a complete wall; the method of setting out is simpler, but just as important. Particular attention must be paid to waterproofing the joint between the tiles and a basin or bath.

Another small area suitable for tiling is a kitchen worktop, which can be tiled to match the splashback behind. Special tiles and grout are needed to produce a sturdy, hygienic surface.

Waterproof seals

When tiling a splashback behind a sink, basin or bath, it is important to ensure a watertight seal along the bottom of the splashback. This will prevent any water from seeping through the joint and running down the wall behind, which could occur even with a waterproof grout.

In most cases, a bead of silicone sealant along the joint between tiles and basin or bath will be sufficient. An alternative is to use plastic sealing strip, which is particularly useful for bridging any slight gap between the bath and wall.

TOOLS: Sealant dispenser, hacksaw, tile saw

MATERIALS: Silicone sealant/plastic sealing strip/quadrant tiles, tile adhesive, grout

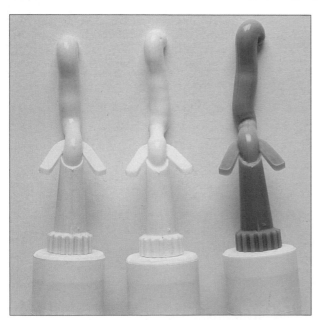

Silicone bath and basin sealants are available in white and a limited range of colours to match common bathroom-suite colours. Some are sold in small syringe-like dispensers that contain enough to run a bead around the average size of bath. Alternatively, you can buy a larger tube for use with a metal, trigger-type dispenser.

If using a trigger dispenser, place the nozzle of the sealant tube at one end of the splashback and apply a smooth bead along its length, squeezing the trigger steadily as you do so. You can smooth any slight irregularities with a finger moistened with water, but take care, as you may ruin the appearance and, worse, the waterproof seal.

QUADRANT TILES

Although not as neat as the plastic sealing strip, quadrant tiles are useful for sealing a gap between a tiled splashback and a bath. The narrow tiles have a curved profile that directs any water back to the bath. They are available in a limited range of colours and sizes.

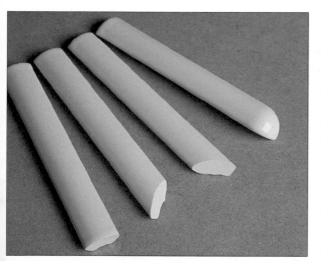

1 Each pack of quadrant tiles should contain square-ended pieces, mitred pieces for corners and bull-nosed stop-ends, together with the necessary adhesive.

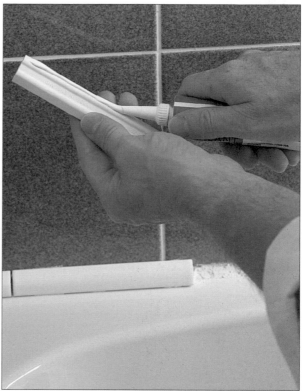

2 Before fitting the quadrant tiles, it is worth sealing the gap between the bath and wall with silicone sealant. If you need to cut a tile to length, use a tile saw. Then fix the tiles with adhesive.

3 Press the quadrant tiles firmly into place. Use tile spacers or pieces of card to space the tiles temporarily while the adhesive sets. Grout all tiles in the normal manner.

PLASTIC SEALING STRIP

This is an L-shaped plastic moulding with a flexible blade along each edge that seals against the wall and against the bath (see pages 70–71). It forms a waterproof seal around a bath while bridging any slight gap between the wall and edge of the bath. Some versions are self-adhesive; others should be bedded in the tile adhesive. In both cases, the tiles are fixed over the vertical half of the strip, although some types are designed so that they can also be fitted afterwards, being stuck to the face of the tiles.

Washbasins

A small area of tiles behind a washbasin may be all that is necessary to protect the wall from splashes. This is particularly the case if the basin is in a cloakroom or a bedroom where a large area of tiles might be considered an inappropriate, 'cold' surface.

Make sure you use tiles with glazed edges, at least around the perimeter of the splashback, as the edges will be visible. Alternatively, you could use proprietary border tiles, tile trim or a painted wooden beading.

TOOLS: Tape measure, pencil, spirit level, small trowel, notched adhesive spreader, grout spreader, sponge, bucket, clean cloth

MATERIALS: Tile adhesive, tiles, tile spacers, water

1 The basin should be level, but you can check with a spirit level to make sure. Any slight deviation from the horizontal can be accommodated by inserting additional cardboard spacers between the tiles and basin (see step 4). The irregular gap can be disguised by silicone sealant. Measure the width of the basin and mark the centre point on the wall behind.

2 There is no need to make a gauge rod for a small job such as this. Instead, you can simply use a tile to measure off the tile positions along the wall, making an allowance for the tile spacers. This will allow you to judge whether your starting point should be in line with the centre point of the basin, or offset to one side of the centre point by half a tile.

3 Having decided on the starting point, use a spirit level to draw a vertical guideline on the wall. This line should extend to the height of the finished splashback. If the basin has a flat upstand, there is no need for a supporting batten; you can tile directly off the basin. Similarly, with such a small area of tiles, there is no need for a vertical batten.

POSITIONING THE TILES

A splashback behind a washbasin is always made up of whole tiles. Small tiles would be a better choice than large ones, as they will be more in scale with the basin.

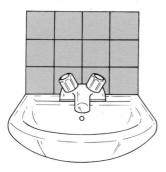
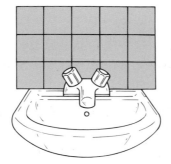

Both the height and width can be varied to suit your needs, but it should be a minimum of 30cm (12in) high to protect the wall from splashing. You may want to extend it higher as a background for a mirror or shelves.

Depending on the size of the tiles, you can make a small splashback by tiling up to the edges of the basin only (left). Alternatively, you can arrange it to project beyond the basin at each end (right). Moving the starting point by half a tile to one side of the basin's centre point may be sufficient for this.

4 Spread adhesive to one side of the guideline, and begin tiling towards the edge of the basin. Set the tiles slightly above the basin on card spacers. When you have tiled one half of the splashback, work in the other direction to complete it. Grout the tiles as normal, but leave the gap between the bottom row of tiles and basin open, as this will be sealed with a silicone sealant.

USING A BATTEN

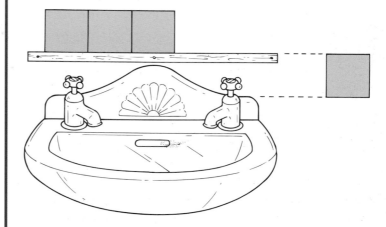

Where the upstand of the basin is not flat, use a batten above the upstand to support all the whole tiles of the splashback.

From the lowest point of the upstand measure vertically up the wall by an amount equal to the height of a tile, including an allowance for grouting. Temporarily nail a horizontal batten to the wall at this point. Tile above the batten using whole tiles. When the adhesive has set, remove the batten and fill in the gap with cut tiles.

Baths

A splashback around a bath may extend around two or even three sides, and is likely to require cut tiles unless it projects beyond the bath at one or both ends. If you would rather keep the splashback to the bath's dimensions and the bath is bounded by two walls, you should tile towards the internal corner, cutting tiles to fit at the corner. If the bath is bounded by three walls, treat the back wall as you would any other (tiling outwards from the centre, with equal cuts at each end) and begin tiling the end walls with a whole tile, working in towards the back wall. The same arrangement is used when tiling a kitchen splashback.

TOOLS: Sealant dispenser, tape measure, pencil, hacksaw, small trowel, notched adhesive spreader, tile spike, steel rule, tile file, grout spreader, sponge, clean cloth, bucket

MATERIALS: Tissue paper, silicone bath sealant, plastic sealing strip, tiles, tile adhesive, tile spacers, grout, water

1 Where a bath is set in the corner of the room, you may find that the walls are not at right-angles, causing a tapered gap between one side of the bath and the wall. In this situation, make sure that the long side of the bath is tight against the wall, as the gap along the short side will be easier to conceal. A very slight deviation could well be hidden by the thickness of the tiles and adhesive, but any significant amount will need concealing with a proprietary sealing strip. Make sure the bath is level before you begin.

2 To make absolutely certain that no water will penetrate the tiles and run down behind the bath, before you add the sealing strip and tiles, fill the gap with silicone sealant. If the gap is quite wide, you may have difficulty in filling it with the sealant, which will tend to fall through. In this situation, wedge in some crumpled tissue paper. This will bridge the gap effectively and provide support for the sealant. Apply a good bead of sealant, adding extra in the corner where the ends of the sealing strip will meet.

PLACING THE TILES

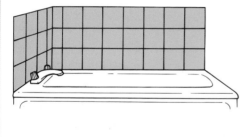

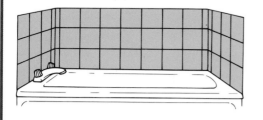

How you position the cut tiles on a splashback for a bath (or kitchen worktop) will depend on whether it occupies two walls or three.

If the splashback is L-shaped, start with a whole tile at each end and work towards the internal corner, where any cuts should be made (left). If the splashback runs around three sides, tile the back wall as normal with equal cuts at each end, but work the ends back from a whole tile towards the internal corners.

ACRYLIC BATHS

If tiling around a modern acrylic bath, fill the bath with water before you fix the tiles to the wall and seal around it. That way, if the bath is likely to become distorted when full, it won't cause any problems with the seal. In fact, this is a wise precaution with any bath.

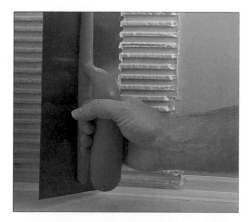

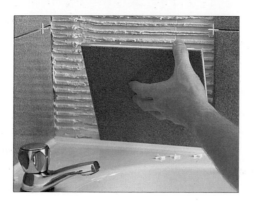

3 Some sealing strips have a self-adhesive backing. Simply peel off the protective paper and press the strip against the wall so that its flexible blade makes a good seal with the top of the bath. Mitre the ends where they meet in the corner, adding more silicone if necessary to ensure a watertight joint. If the strip has no self-adhesive backing, bed it in tile adhesive.

4 Having set out the splashback and decided on a starting point, spread a layer of adhesive on the wall. Work on a small area at a time to ensure that the adhesive remains workable. Make sure it overlaps the sealing strip completely.

5 Add the tiles, working towards the corner if the bath is bounded by two walls. Make sure the tiles are bedded properly, and add spacers to ensure uniform grout gaps. Grout the tiles in the normal manner.

Worktops

Although the wide range of laminated worktops for kitchens has made tiled worktops less popular, tiling remains a viable method of providing a tough, hygienic surface, which looks particularly effective in period- and rustic-style kitchens. However, normal ceramic wall tiles are not suitable for use on worktops: they are not strong enough to withstand hot pans and the kind of wear and tear that a kitchen worktop receives. Use worktop tiles which are designed for the job.

If you want the splashback and worktop to match, you will have to use the same tiles on the wall. Another important consideration is the grout used, which must be an epoxy type for a kitchen.

TOOLS: Hammer, saw, small trowel, notched adhesive spreader, wooden straight edge, tape measure, felt-tip pen/chinagraph pencil, tile cutting machine, filling knife, plastic scouring pad, sponge, bucket

MATERIALS: Wooden beading, nails, tile adhesive, tiles, epoxy grout, water

PLANNING AND SETTING OUT

Although you can give an existing worktop a facelift by tiling, it is much better to begin with a fresh surface. Use marine-grade plywood at least 13mm (½in) thick. If you intend attaching this to existing cabinets, you will not need to provide any additional support; otherwise it must be strengthened by screwing battens to the underside,

around the edges and across the width at 600mm (24in) intervals.

Where possible, adjust the width and length of the board so that you will not have to cut any tiles. If you do have to cut tiles to fit, use a tile-cutting machine, as they will be too hard to break by scoring and snapping with hand tools.

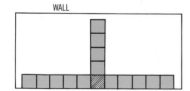

Straight worktop
If a straight worktop is to be tiled and it is set against the back wall only, begin tiling in the centre, at the front. If necessary, insert equal-sized cut tiles at each end.

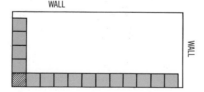

Top bounded by two walls
If the worktop is straight, begin with a whole tile at the front corner and work towards each wall, fitting cut tiles at the walls as necessary.

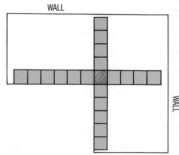

L-shaped worktop
Begin at the corner of the two surfaces with a whole tile. Work towards each end and the walls.

FIXING THE TILES

1 Begin by pinning wooden beading around the worktop, setting its height to match the thickness of the tiles. If you intend staining the beading, do this before laying the tiles.

Spread adhesive on the worktop using the notched spreader. Cover an area of no more than 1sq m (1sq yd) at a time.

Lay the tiles, using pieces of card no more than 3mm (⅛in) thick for spacers. Some worktop tiles come in panels on a mesh backing, which takes care of the spacing for you. With these, you must make sure that each tile is firmly bedded in the adhesive by pressing down with a grout spreader or similar tool.

2 Periodically check that the tiles are level by holding a wooden straight edge across them. Any tiles that are too high or too low should be lifted carefully and bedded on fresh adhesive.

3 Any cut tiles should be inserted where the worktop meets the wall. If you are left with an impossibly small gap to fill, you can conceal it with a decorative wooden moulding or proprietary worktop upstand.

GROUTING

When tiling a kitchen worktop, you must use a two-part epoxy grout. This is not only waterproof and stain-resistant, but also hygienic, as it will not harbour germs. It is essential to work quickly when using epoxy grout, as it hardens rapidly and can be extremely difficult to remove from the face of the tiles.

1 Epoxy grout is much stiffer than normal grout and must be applied in a different manner. Apply it directly to the joints with a filling knife.

2 As soon as you have filled all the joints, gently rub over the surface of the tiles with a wet plastic kitchen scouring pad. This will remove any residue from the tiles and smooth the grout between them. By keeping the pad flat, you won't run the risk of dragging any of the grout from the joints.

Finally, sponge off the surface of the tiles and then allow the grout to harden for the specified amount of time before using the worktop.

Mosaics and Marbles

Mosaics are much smaller than normal wall tiles, usually 25–50mm (1–2in) square. Because of this they are supplied in sheets, either on a mesh backing or with a paper facing. The size of sheet will vary depending on the size of the individual tiles, which may be glazed ceramic or glass.

Although mosaics can be used in the same manner as normal wall tiles, they are usually best restricted to small areas such as splashbacks, as their small size can make a large area look very busy. Due to their small size they are ideal for tiling curved surfaces; sheets can easily be wrapped around a curve without the joints between the tiles opening up too much.

Marble tiles are much more expensive than normal ceramic tiles, but they bring a unique quality to a tiled surface. They are completely flat, and with flush-grouted joints produce a smooth, elegant finish.

Setting out mosaics

The method of setting out for mosaics is essentially the same as for any wall tiles, and for a large area it will pay to make up a gauge rod, marked off in panel widths and lengths. It is important to remember that you can cut strips of mosaics from the sheets to fill in at the ends of rows, but since the individual tiles are quite small you may encounter problems if you have to cut the tiles themselves.

TOOLS: Tape measure, pencil, spirit level

MATERIALS: Mosaic sheets

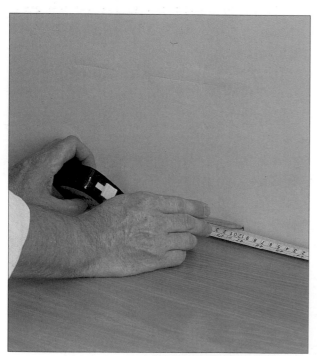

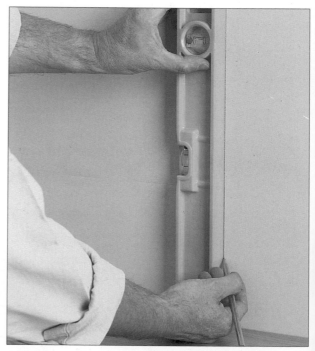

1 Find the centre of the area to be tiled by measuring, and mark the point with a pencil. Although you can use mosaics to tile a complete wall, they are more appropriate for use on smaller areas, such as this splashback behind a kitchen worktop. Since the worktop should be level, you can work directly from it rather than using a support batten.

2 Use a spirit level to extend the pencil mark vertically on the wall. Make the line the height of the proposed splashback. Ideally, this should be equal to a number of whole sheets; if not, a number of whole tiles. If the splashback is between a worktop and cupboards above, place any cut tiles at the very top where they will be concealed by the overhanging cupboards.

3 If you are tiling a small area, like this wall behind a worktop, there is no need to make a gauge rod; simply use a sheet of mosaics to mark the positions along the wall. Remember to allow the same gap between each sheet as between the individual tiles.

4 At each end, you may find that you only need part of a sheet to finish off, possibly with a row of cut tiles in the corner. Because of their small size, any cut tiles should be at least half a tile wide. The gap shown is too narrow to fill easily, as cutting the thin slivers of tile would be very difficult.

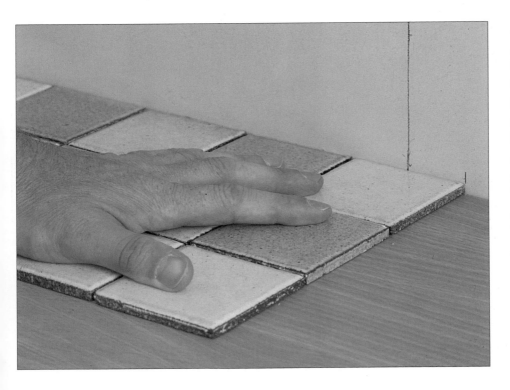

5 To overcome very narrow cut tiles at each end of the splashback, reposition the starting point by half a tile to one side and draw a fresh vertical line. There is no need for a vertical guide batten when tiling a splashback, especially with sheets of mosaics, but for a larger area you may prefer to nail one in place temporarily.

Fixing mosaics

The techniques for fixing mosaic sheets to the wall are very similar to those used for ordinary tiles. However, you must make a special effort to ensure that all the individual tiles are bedded firmly in the adhesive. Since the tiles are small, pressing each one into the adhesive is not a practical proposition. A much more effective solution is to use a grout spreader or wooden tamping block, working across each sheet with a firm slapping action, pressing down several tiles at each blow.

Correct spacing of the sheets is also important and it must match the spacing between the tiles on the sheet. Use pieces of card of the correct thickness to achieve this.

TOOLS: Small trowel, notched adhesive spreader, grout spreader, plasterer's trowel, spirit level, long wooden straight edge

MATERIALS: Mosaic sheets, tile adhesive, card for spacers

1 Having determined the starting point, spread adhesive on the wall, sufficient to fix three or four sheets of the mosaic tiles.

2 Press the first sheet of tiles into the adhesive, aligning its side edge carefully with the vertical pencil line.

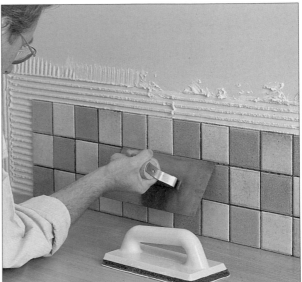

3 Use a float-type grout spreader to bed the tiles in the adhesive, working across the sheet with a slapping action and delivering light, but firm, blows. This also ensures that the mesh backing is stretched out fully so that the gaps between the tiles will be uniform.

4 Take care to keep the sheets aligned so that the horizontal joints are continuous. One way of checking the alignment is to hold the edge of a plasterer's trowel against the underside of each row of tiles, pressing upwards lightly if necessary to bring the sheets into line.

ARRANGING THE SHEETS

Quite often, sheets of mosaics are made up of tiles in several different colours arranged in a random pattern.

With very small mosaics, this may be truly random with each sheet being different from the next. However, with larger mosaics, the tiles may be arranged in the same pattern on each sheet or, in each box, there may be sheets with two or three different arrangements. It is worth checking for this, as the sheets may look better one way than another.

You can even have a trial run of the final result by laying out several sheets on the floor. Even with a random arrangement of tiles, you should still aim for a balanced appearance to the overall job.

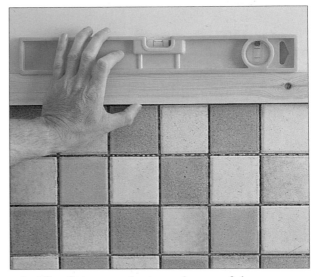

5 After fixing two horizontal rows of sheets, use a spirit level and long wooden straight edge to check that they are level and in line. Make any adjustments as necessary. Continue adding sheets in this way until you have covered the bulk of the wall.

Cutting in

The small size of mosaics means that in many cases you will not have to cut any tiles at the ends of rows to complete the job. However, if you can't avoid cutting tiles, you will have to remove them individually from the sheets, measure the gaps to be filled and then cut the tiles accordingly. With larger mosaics, you may find a combined wheel cutter/snapper will work well; alternatively, scoring the tile and breaking off the waste with a pair of nibblers is best for smaller mosaics.

TOOLS: Craft knife, notched adhesive spreader, tape measure, felt-tip pen/chinagraph pencil, steel rule, tile spike and nibblers or wheel cutter/snapper

MATERIALS: Mosaic sheets, tile adhesive

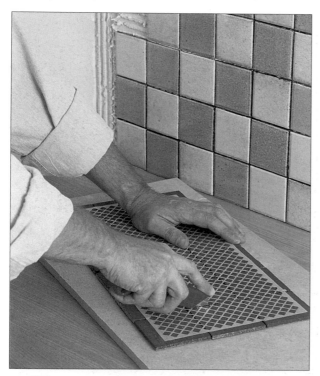

1 When you reach the end of the splashback, cut individual strips of tiles from the sheets as necessary to fill the remaining gap. Place the sheet face down and cut through the mesh backing with a sharp knife.

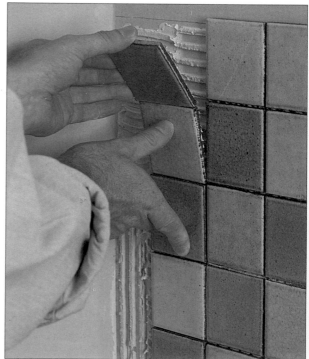

2 Remove any projecting portions of the paper backing from the strips of tiles. Then spread a layer of adhesive on the wall and press the tiles into place, bedding them firmly and aligning them carefully with their neighbours.

CROOKED TILES

Occasionally you may find that a tile is out of place or crooked in the sheet. If you notice this before you fix the sheet to the wall, you can cut the tile out and fix it separately. If the crooked tile is only apparent after the sheet is on the wall, you will have to free the tile from its backing and twist it back into line.

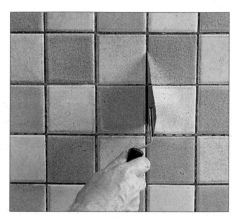

1 If a tile is noticeably crooked after you have fixed a sheet, cut through the backing on all four sides with a craft knife.

2 Taking care not to knock it off the wall, use a small trowel to lever the tile gently back into line with its neighbours.

3 If you need to cut some tiles to fill in any remaining space, remove them individually from the sheet. Measure and mark them as you would a normal size tile, then score and snap them or nibble off the waste.

4 Press the individual cut tiles into place to fill the remaining gap in the corner. Since they will not benefit from the automatic spacing provided by the backing mesh, you will need to add spacers, such as pieces of cardboard, between them.

Grouting

As with all tiles, the joints between mosaics need grouting. However, because the individual tiles are much smaller and, therefore, there are many more joints, shaping them could be a time-consuming task, and you could find the grout beginning to harden before you completed it. Consequently, after applying the grout, it is better just to sponge the mosaics to leave the grout flush with the edges of the tiles. Since these are usually bevelled slightly to produce a V-shaped joint, you will achieve a neat finish with little effort.

TOOLS: Small trowel, grout spreader, sponge, soft cloth, bucket

MATERIALS: Grout, water

1 Scoop up some grout with a small trowel and press it on to the face of the mosaic. Spread it with the grout spreader, pressing it into the joints. Hold the blade of the spreader at an angle, working it diagonally across the joints to ensure that they are full, but keeping as much grout as possible off the face of the tiles.

2 Wipe over the tiles with a damp sponge to remove the excess grout and smooth the joints. Rinse the sponge regularly in clean water. Take care, however, not to drag grout from the joints by pressing too hard. When the grout has dried, polish the powdery film from the face of the tiles with a soft, clean cloth.

PAPER-FACED MOSAICS

1 Some small mosaics, such as these glass examples, come with a paper facing sheet that holds them together rather than a mesh backing. They are fixed to the wall in exactly the same way as mesh-backed types, being bedded by slapping with a grout spreader. After allowing the adhesive to dry, soak the paper facings of the mosaic panels with a wet sponge. Make sure that each sheet of paper is soaked completely and thoroughly.

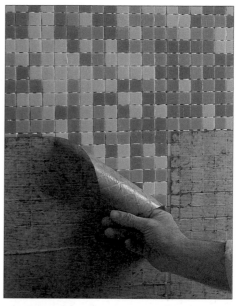

2 Wait for a few minutes for the water to soak into the paper, then peel off each sheet.

3 Wash the tiles down with a sponge and clean water to remove all traces of the paper adhesive. Then spread grout over the mosaic panels, making sure you fill all the joints. Using a sponge to remove excess grout can drag it from the joints; it is better to let it dry slightly, then wipe off the excess with a damp cloth. When the grout has dried completely, polish off the tiles in the normal manner.

Marble tiles

Although marble tiles are fixed to the wall in a similar manner to ceramic tiles, there are some important points to consider if you are to achieve a good finish. Marble tiles are perfectly flat with square-cut edges, and look best if fixed with very narrow joints between them. In addition, they are translucent, and any irregular colouring of the wall may show through a pale coloured tile. Finally, although the material is not difficult to cut, it is best to use a tile-cutting machine rather than a tile spike and attempting to snap them by hand. The reason is that marble tiles do not always cut as cleanly as ceramic types and the machine will produce a better cut. The cut edges can easily be cleaned up with silicone carbide paper.

TOOLS: Paintbrush, tape measure, pencil, spirit level, gauge rod, small trowel, notched adhesive spreader, grout spreader, sponge, clean cloth, bucket, felt-tip pen/chinagraph pencil, tile-cutting machine

MATERIALS: PVA sealer, white emulsion paint, wooden battens, masonry nails, marble tiles, tile adhesive, grout, water

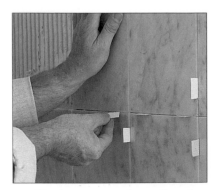

1 Having set out the wall and fixed the guide battens, you can begin to fix the marble tiles in the same manner as ceramic tiles. However, they look best if the joints between them are kept as thin as possible – about 1–2mm (1⁄16in) – so rather than use conventional tile spacers, insert pieces of thin card instead.

2 You can treat external corners in the same way as ceramic tiles, by overlapping the edges, but for the best effect, the edges of the tiles should be mitred. Many tile suppliers will mitre the tiles for you; failing that, you can hire a saw table with a diamond-tipped blade and do the job yourself.

3 As with other forms of tiling, complete the main wall first, then the return wall, working away from the external corner. Position the corner tiles carefully, inserting thin pieces of cardboard between the mitred faces to maintain the correct spacing. This will leave a neat joint at the apex of the corner.

4 As they are perfectly flat, it is essential that the faces of the tiles are flush. Otherwise, the look of the job will be spoiled. As you are working, periodically hold a wooden straight edge across the faces of the tiles to check for any that are too high or too low.

5 If necessary, carefully remove any of the tiles that are out of line, scrape off the old adhesive and apply a fresh coating to the back of the tile, rather than the wall. Refit the tile in its space and check that it is completely level with the surrounding tiles using the straight edge.

6 When you begin to grout the tiles, fill the joints of the external corners first. Hold the grout spreader at an angle and with a little grout on the edge of the blade, press it gently into the corner joint. Then gently draw the blade up the corner to scrape off any excess.

7 Grout the rest of the tiles in the normal manner, working the blade of the spreader diagonally across the joints, rather than along them to prevent any of the grout from being dragged out again.

8 As grout must be flush with the tiles, do not use a sponge to wash off excess. Wait for it to stiffen slightly, then wipe off the excess with a cloth. For this reason, try to keep grout off the face of the tiles when grouting.

PAINTING THE WALL

When sealing the wall prior to tiling, it is a good idea to mix the sealer with white emulsion paint if you will be fixing pale-coloured tiles. This will prevent any dark-coloured areas on the wall showing through the tiles once they are in place.

Dilute the PVA sealant in accordance with the maker's instructions, then add the white emulsion, mixing it with between one quarter and half as much paint as sealer, and apply this mixture to the wall. Leave to dry completely.

Renovation and Repair

Tiles provide a long-lasting surface which is easily cleaned and will keep its good looks for many years.

However, as with any decorative finish, time can take its toll on appearance. Grout can become stained and discoloured – even if the tiles are washed down regularly – while the tiles themselves may become cracked or broken from accidental knocks.

When refurbishing a kitchen or bathroom, you may find that you are left with unsightly screw holes in tiles where wall-mounted fittings have been removed and not replaced; or you may inherit a tiled surface in poor condition when buying a house.

While there is not much that you can do about poor-quality and uneven tiling short of stripping it off and starting afresh, you can replace grout that has seen better days and tiles that have become damaged. Both jobs are quite simple to do and are well worth the effort, making your tiles look like new.

This chapter contains

Renewing grout

Over the years, grout can become discoloured and stained, particularly where the tiles are subjected to high levels of moisture, such as in a shower or around a bath. If the ventilation is poor, they take a long time to dry out. Eventually, this can lead to the growth of black mould, which is difficult to remove.

Fortunately, it is an easy situation to remedy. Essentially, all that is necessary is to rake out all of the old grout and replace it with fresh. Doing this will make even an old tiled surface look like new.

TOOLS: Grout raker, small trowel, grout spreader, sponge, grout shaper, clean cloth, bucket

MATERIALS: Grout, water

1 Use a proper grout raker to remove the old grout from around the tiles, taking care not to damage their edges. Do all the vertical joints, then the horizontal joints, or vice versa, so that you don't miss any. Make sure you remove the grout down to at least half the thickness of the tile.

2 Press some fresh grout on to the face of the tiles with a small trowel, then spread it over the tiles, pressing it into the joints. Move the spreader diagonally over the joints rather than along them to prevent the grout from being dragged out again. Carry on until all the joints have been filled.

CLEANING FLUIDS

Minor staining and fungal growths can be removed from grout using a proprietary grout cleaner. This will contain a variety of detergents and biological agents to clean the grout and discourage further mould growth.

The normal procedure is to dilute the cleaner with an equal amount of warm water, then apply it to the grout with a brush or sponge. After you have allowed the fluid to dry, any residue can be rinsed off and the tiles dried with an absorbent cloth.

3 Use a wet sponge to wash all the excess grout from the face of the tiles, but don't press too hard as you may remove it from the joints as well. Then allow the grout to harden slightly.

4 Run a grout shaper along the joints to give them the correct profile, or use a large-diameter wooden dowel. Any grout that squeezes out should be removed with the sponge.

IDEAL TOOLS

Grout is designed to provide a hard filling for the joints between tiles, so it needs a little effort to remove. The only way this can be done is to scrape it out with a sharp, pointed tool. While you may be able to improvise a tool for the job, you must take care not to damage the tiles themselves, and it is best to use a proper grout raker that has been designed for the job.

Grout rakers come in various forms. The toothed version on the left has a thin blade suitable for narrow joints, while the tool on the right will cope with wider joints. The latter can also be used for scoring tiles prior to cutting them.

5 Allow the grout to dry, then polish off the powdery film from the face of the tiles with a soft, clean cloth.

Replacing a damaged tile

Over the years, ceramic wall tiles may become damaged from accidental blows, or you may find that changing bathroom or kitchen fittings leaves some tiles with unsightly screw holes that cannot be filled in a satisfactory manner.

Such damage will disfigure a tiled surface and, where the tiles are used as a splashback or surround for a shower, can allow water to seep through to the wall behind with potentially disastrous results. In a kitchen, a cracked or broken tile can harbour dirt and germs, which is definitely not desirable.

Fortunately, replacing a damaged tile is quite a straightforward operation.

TOOLS: Grout raker, electric drill, ceramic tile/masonry bit, cold chisel, hammer, thick gloves, goggles, small trowel, notched adhesive spreader, straight wooden batten, grout spreader, sponge, grout shaper, clean cloth, bucket

MATERIALS: Tile, tile adhesive, tile spacers, grout, water

IDEAL TOOL

A ceramic tile drill bit is designed to bite immediately into the glaze of a tile without skidding, removing the need for masking tape or breaking through the glaze with a sharp pointed tool. Various sizes of bit are available to suit a range of hole diameters.

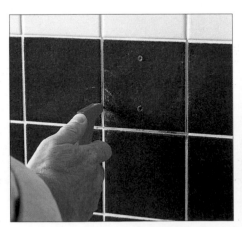

1 In this case, a tile is being replaced after a wall-mounted fitting has been removed, exposing two unsightly screw holes. The first job is to rake out the grout completely on all four sides of the tile.

2 Drill a series of holes around the centre of the tile, using a ceramic tile bit and an electric drill. Since the tile is being removed, even a masonry bit can be used without tape, as if it slips slightly it will not matter.

3 Use a hammer and cold chisel to cut through the tile between the holes and chop out the central portion of the tile. Wear thick gloves to protect your hands and goggles to shield your eyes from flying fragments, which can be sharp.

4 Work carefully towards the edges of the tile, gently breaking pieces away. Be very careful when you get close to the neighbouring tiles, as a slip could mean replacing more than one. With the tile removed, chisel out as much adhesive as possible.

5 Check that you have removed enough adhesive by inserting the dry tile and noting how it sits in relation to the surrounding tiles: it must not stand proud of them. Then coat the back of the tile with adhesive and set it in place.

A SUITABLE REPLACEMENT

Finding a replacement for a broken tile can present a problem, unless you have some spares left over from when the job was done originally. This is a good reason for ordering a few more tiles than you actually need for a job and keeping the extras.

If the tiles are very old, or you don't know the source or manufacturer, you may not be able to match what you have. In a situation like this, the best you can do is look for an inset tile of the same size to drop in, perhaps removing a few other tiles at random to fit similar tiles. That way, the repair won't be so obvious and you can give your tiles a new look at the same time.

Alternatively, you could remove several tiles around the broken one and insert a picture or feature panel of some sort. Although this can involve a considerable amount of work, it is the only way that you will effectively overcome the lack of an identical replacement.

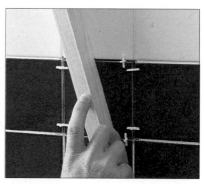

6 Press the tile into place with the aid of a wooden batten. This will ensure that it is flush with the adjacent tiles. Fit tile spacers to ensure uniform grout joints. When the adhesive has set, remove the spacers and grout the tile in the usual manner.

Glossary

Biscuit

The clay body of a tile to which a liquid ceramic glaze is applied. The tile is then 'fired' under intense heat in a kiln to set the glaze into a very hard surface. Patterned tiles may be fired several times, each part of the pattern being added separately.

Border tile

A tile designed specifically for edging an area of tiles. Usually narrower than standard tiles, normally coloured or patterned, and with their outer edge glazed to provide a neat finish.

Corner trim

A moulded plastic strip designed for finishing an external corner where two tiled walls meet. Corner trim is essential when using tiles with unglazed edges. Various colours are available, as are several sizes to accommodate different thicknesses of tile.

Cutting in

Cutting tiles to fit a narrow gap at the end of a row (where it meets an adjacent wall, for example). Any cut tiles of this type should be at least half a tile wide. This avoids the need to cut thin slivers of tile.

Dado

A horizontal row of tiles or a wooden moulding running across a wall at waist height; used to break up a large expanse of tiles or to provide a break between one tiling layout and another.

Field tiles

Standard, uncut tiles used to fill the central portion of a tiled area.

Gauge rod

A wooden batten marked off at intervals that correspond to the width of the tiles being used (with an allowance for grout joints). It is used to determine where the horizontal and vertical rows of tiles will fall on the wall, indicating the width of any necessary cut tiles at the ends of rows. It also helps determine the best point to begin tiling.

Grout

Fills the joints between tiles, providing a very hard finish. Some grouts are completely waterproof, while epoxy grout is also hygienic and safe for use on kitchen worktops.

Grout raker

A rigid-bladed tool for scraping out old cracked and discoloured grout prior to renewing the grout or removing a damaged tile.

Grout shaper

A plastic tool for giving a neat, slightly recessed finish to grout joints while the grout is still soft.

Insert

A small square tile inserted at the point where the corners of four larger tiles would normally meet.

Inset tile

A standard-size tile with a central motif used to provide visual

interest in a large expanse of single-colour tiles. Insets can be fixed at random throughout the tiled area or in a definite pattern.

Mitred
Cut at an angle of 45 degrees. Border tiles can have their adjacent ends mitred when framing a splashback to ensure continuation of the pattern from horizontal to vertical.

Mosaics
Small tiles in sheet form with a mesh backing or paper facing.

Nibblers
Used for breaking off small amounts of waste when making a cut-out in a tile or removing a narrow strip. Special narrow-jawed versions are available for working in a confined space.

Pencil tile
A very narrow tile, not much wider than a pencil, with a rounded face normally used in conjunction with dado tiles.

Picture tiles
Groups of tiles that fit together to make a larger picture. They can be used much like an inset to break up a large expanse of tiles.

Profile gauge
A special tool for copying the shapes of objects and transferring them to tiles for cutting.

Quadrant tile
A narrow rounded tile for fitting at the junction of a tiled splashback and a bath or basin.

Reveal
The narrow return strips of a wall around a recessed window.

Setting out
Marking the wall with the starting point for tiling and fitting guide battens (if needed) for the tiles. Normally, you begin tiling at the centre of the wall and work towards the ends.

Squeegee
Term used for grout spreader, tool used for spreading grout.

Template
A pattern (normally paper) used to copy the shape of an item and transfer it to a tile for cutting.

Tile file
A special file for cleaning up the edges of tiles after they have been cut. Some have both flat and curved faces, allowing straight and curved cuts to be dressed.

Tile scorer
A tool with a narrow, hardened, chisel-like blade for scoring the glaze of a tile prior to snapping it in two. Without this, it is impossible to produce a clean, straight break.

Tile spike
A pencil-like version of the tile scorer with a needle-like tip. Easier to use than the chisel type, since its tip will sit tightly against the edge of a steel rule for greater accuracy when scoring.

Upstand
A vertical surface at the back of a washbasin designed to prevent water splashing against the wall.

Index

The author and publisher would like to thank the
following for their assistance in producing this book:

World's End Tiles, London (technical assistance, tools and materials)

Paul Tebano, Tebano Tiling, Yeovil (technical assistance)
C P Hart, London (location facilities)

Editor:	Margot Richardson
Designers:	Hilary Prosser and John Round
Project co-ordinator:	Ian Penberthy
Managing Editor:	Miranda Spicer
Art Director:	Martin Lovelock
Photography:	Nick Pope
'Ideas and Choices' stylist:	Sarah Hollywood
Illustrator:	David Eaton
Production Manager:	Kevin Perrett
Set Builder:	Nigel Tate

Alex Portelli has asserted her right to be identified as the author of this work.

Reprinted 1996/1998

Published by: Haynes Publishing
Sparkford, Nr Yeovil, Somerset BA22 7JJ

British Library Cataloguing-in-Publication Data:
A catalogue record for this book is available from the British Library.

ISBN 1 85960 108 1

Printed in France by
Imprimerie Pollina, 85400 Luçon - n° 76173